SYMBOLS AND VALUES IN ZOROASTRIANISM

Their Survival and Renewal

RELIGIOUS PERSPECTIVES • VOLUME FIFTEEN

SYMBOLS AND VALUES
IN ZOROASTRIANISM
Their Survival and Renewal

Jacques Duchesne-Guillemin

HARPER AND ROW, PUBLISHERS

New York

Contents

v

RELIGIOUS PERSPECTIVES

VOLUMES ALREADY PUBLISHED

ix

RELIGIOUS PERSPECTIVES

Its Meaning and Purpose

Religious Perspectives represents a quest for the rediscovery of man. It constitutes an effort to define man's search for the essence of being in order that he may have a knowledge of goals. It is an endeavor to show that there is no possibility of achieving an understanding of man's total nature on the basis of phenomena known by the analytical method alone. It hopes to point to the false antimony between revelation and reason, faith and knowledge, grace and nature, courage and anxiety. Mathematics, physics, philosophy, biology, and religion, in spite of their almost complete independence, have begun to sense their interrelatedness and to become aware of that mode of cognition which teaches that "the light is not without but within me, and I myself am the light."

Modern man is threatened by a world created by himself. He is faced with the conversion of mind to naturalism, a dogmatic secularism and an opposition to a belief in the transcendent. He begins to see, however, that the universe is given not as one existing and one perceived but as the unity of subject and object; that the barrier between them cannot be said to have been dissolved as the result of recent experience in the physical sciences, since this barrier has never existed. Confronted with the question of meaning, he is summoned to rediscover and scrutinize the immutable and the permanent which constitute the dynamic, unifying aspect of life as well as the principle of differentiation; to reconcile identity and diversity, immutability and unrest. He begins to recognize that just as every person descends by his particular path, so he is able to ascend, and this ascent aims at a return to the source of creation, an inward home from which he has become estranged.

It is the hope of Religious Perspectives that the rediscovery of man will point the way to the rediscovery of God. To this end a rediscovery of first principles should constitute part of the quest. These principles, not to be superseded by new discoveries, are not those of historical worlds that come to be and perish. They are to be sought in the heart and spirit of man, and no interpretation of a merely historical or scientific universe can guide the search. Religious Perspectives attempts not only to ask dispassionately what the nature of God is, but also to restore to human life at least the hypothesis of God and the symbols that relate to him. It endeavors to show that man is faced with the metaphysical question of the truth of religion while he encounters the empirical question of its effects on the life of humanity and its meaning for society. Religion is here distinguished from theology and its doctrinal forms and is intended to denote the feelings, aspirations, and acts of men, as they relate to total reality.

Religious Perspectives is nourished by the spiritual and intellectual energy of world thought, by those religious and ethical leaders who are not merely spectators but scholars deeply involved in the critical problems common to all religions. These thinkers recognize that human morality and human ideals thrive only when set in a context of a transcendent attitude toward religion and that by pointing to the ground of identity and the common nature of being in the religious experience of man, the essential nature of religion may be defined. Thus, they are committed to re-evaluate the meaning of everlastingness, an experience which has been lost and which is the content of that *visio Dei* constituting the structure of all religions. It is the many absorbed everlastingly into the ultimate unity, a unity subsuming what Whitehead calls the fluency of God and the everlastingness of passing experience.

These volumes seek to show that the unity of which we speak consists in a certitude emanating from the nature of man who seeks God and the nature of God who seeks man. Such certitude bathes in an intuitive act of cognition, participating in the divine essence and is related to the natural sprituality of intelligence. This is not by any means to say that there is an equivalence of all faiths in the traditional religions of human history. It is, however, to emphasize the distinction between the spiritual and the temporal which all religions acknowledge. For duration of thought is composed of instants superior to time, and is an intuition of the permanence of existence and is metahistorical reality. In fact, the symbol[1] itself found on cover and jacket of each volume of Religious Perspectives is the visible sign or representation of the essence, immediacy, and timelessness of religious experience; the one immutable center, which may be analogically related to Being in pure act, moving with centrifugal and ecumenical necessity outward into the manifold modes, yet simultaneously, with dynamic centripetal power and with full intentional energy, returning to the source. Through the very diversity of its authors, the Series shows that the basic and poignant concern of every faith is to point to, and overcome the crisis in our apocalyptic epoch—the crisis of man's separa-

---

[1] From the original design by Leo Katz.

tion from man and of man's separation from God—the failure
of love. The authors endeavor, moreover, to illustrate the
truth that the human heart is able, and even yearns, to go to
the very lengths of God; that the darkness and cold, the frozen
spiritual misery of recent time, are breaking, cracking, and
beginning to move, yielding to efforts to overcome spiritual
muteness and moral paralysis. In this way, it is hoped, the
immediacy of pain and sorrow, the primacy of tragedy and
suffering in human life, may be transmuted into a spiritual
and moral triumph.

Religious Perspectives is therefore an effort to explore the
meaning of God, an exploration which constitutes an aspect of
man's intrinsic nature, part of his ontological substance. The
Series grows out of an abiding concern that in spite of the
release of man's creative energy which science has in part
accomplished, this very science has overturned the essential
order of nature. Shrewd as man's calculations have become
concerning his means, his choice of ends which was formerly
correlated with belief in God, with absolute criteria of conduct, has become witless. God is not to be treated as an
exception to metaphysical principles, invoked to prevent their
collapse. He is rather their chief exemplification, the source of
all potentiality. The personal reality of freedom and providence, of will and conscience, may demonstrate that "he who
knows" commands a depth of consciousness inaccessible to the
profane man, and is capable of that transfiguration which
prevents the twisting of all good to ignominy. This religious
content of experience is not within the province of science to
bestow; it corrects the error of treating the scientific account
as if it were itself metaphysical or religious; it challenges the

tendency to make a religion of science—or a science of religion—a dogmatic act which destroys the moral dynamic of man. Indeed, many men of science are confronted with unexpected implications of their own thought and are beginning to accept, for instance, the trans-spatial and trans-temporal dimension in the nature of reality.

Religious Perspectives attempts to show the fallacy of the apparent irrelevance of God in history. The Series submits that no convincing image of man can arise, in spite of the many ways in which human thought has tried to reach it, without a philosophy of human nature and human freedom which does not exclude God. This image of *Homo cum Deo* implies the highest conceivable freedom, the freedom to step into the very fabric of the universe, a new formula for man's collaboration with the creative process and the only one which is able to protect man from the terror of existence. This image implies further that the mind and conscience are capable of making genuine discriminations and thereby may reconcile the serious tensions between the secular and religious, the profane and sacred. The idea of the sacred lies in what it *is,* timeless existence. By emphasizing timeless existence against reason as a reality, we are liberated, in our communion with the eternal, from the otherwise unbreakable rule of "before and after." Then we are able to admit that all forms, all symbols in religions, by their negation of error and their affirmation of the actuality of truth, make it possible to experience that *knowing* which is above knowledge, and that dynamic passage of the universe to unending unity.

The volumes in this Series seek to challenge the crisis which separates, to make reasonable a religion that binds, and to present the numinous reality within the experience of man. Insofar as the Series succeeds in this quest, it will direct mankind toward a reality that is eternal and away from a preoccupation with that which is illusory and ephemeral.

God is here interpreted not as a heteronomous being issuing commandments but as the *Tat-tram-asi:* "Do unto others as you would have others do unto you. For I am the Lord." This does not mean a commandment but rather a self-realization through "the other"; since the isolated individual is unthinkable and meaningless. Man becomes man by recognizing his true nature as a creature capable of self-transcendence. For then the divine and the sacred become manifest. And though he believes in choices, he is no Utopian expecting the "coming of the kingdom." Man, individually and collectively, is losing the chains which have bound him to the inexorable demands of nature. The constraints are diminishing and an infinity of choices become available to him. Thus man himself, from the sources of his ontological being, at last must decide what is the *bonum et malum.* And though the anonymous forces which in the past have set the constraints do indeed threaten him with total anarchy and with perhaps a worse tyranny than he experienced in past history, he nevertheless begins to see that preceding the moral issue is the cognitive problem: the perception of those conditions for life which permit mankind to fulfill itself and to accept the truth that beyond scientific, discursive knowledge there is nondiscursive intuitive awareness. And, I suggest, this is not to secularize God but rather to gather him into the heart of the nature of matter, and indeed of life itself.

For man is now confronted with his burden and his greatness: "He calleth to me, Watchman, what of the night?

Watchman, what of the night?"[1] Perhaps the anguish in the human soul may be assuaged by the answer, by the *assimilation* of the person in God: "The morning cometh, and also the night: if ye will inquire, inquire ye: return, come."[2]

RUTH NANDA ANSHEN

[1] Isaiah 21:11.
[2] Isaiah 21:12.

SYMBOLS AND VALUES IN ZOROASTRIANISM
Their Survival and Renewal

Introduction

The Parsees number a little over 115,000, and live in Bombay and in a few towns and villages, mostly north of Bombay. Although they are not, strictly speaking, a caste, since they do not belong to Hinduism, they are a well-defined community.

They were among the first to open themselves up to European influence—under the British rule—and this was one of the reasons for their prosperity. On the other hand, they remain a closed community, not only in that they never marry outside of it, but also in that, clinging to the beliefs and customs of their ancestors as to so many distinctive marks, they do not seek to spread them.

As their name shows, they descend from Persian immigrants. In them, as well as in their ten thousand cousins who have remained in Iran (in the regions of Kerman and Yazd), the old religion lives on, which was that of the whole of Iran until the Arab conquest. They claim allegiance to the god Mazda or Ormazd (Ormuzd) and to his prophet Zoroaster (Zardusht, Zarathushtra). The most conspicuous traits of their religion are the cult of Fire and the Towers of Silence.

For a long time under their Hindu prince, then under his Muslim successor, they were simple farmers, until by the time of the arrival of the English, with whom they were to become the best collaborators, they took to commerce. They have been called the Jews of India. Then it was that they began to settle down in Bombay and Bombay began to grow. Previously their centers had been successively Sanjan, Nausari, Surat, Bulsar, Udvada. Surat was still their main town when Anquetil visited them in the eighteenth century. From the middle of the nineteenth century onward, whatever was founded in India in the way of shipbuilding, railroads, iron mills, etc., was their work.

They were distinguished for their beneficence and their education, as well as for their wealth, striving as they were to alleviate misery without distinction of race or religion, founding hospitals, orphanages, schools. They had once adopted from their Hindu environment a new language (Gujarati) and a new costume. Though they felt the attraction of astrology and mysticism, these could not prevail over their traditional religion, which was equally distant from fatalism and asceticism. They succeeded in adopting the English manners, the European costume, the education of women, the abolition of infant marriage. In their enterprises as well as in their charity, they were following the Western example. Several of them were knighted by the British Crown. There was one Parsee baronet, two Parsee Members of Parliament.

What caused the Parsees to excel in this way? An American geographer, Elsworth Huntington of Yale, studying the general effect of race and environment on the development of civilization, cites the Parsees as typical of a community tried but fortified by natural selection, which allows only the fittest to survive. It had required some courage to escape Islam; then, in the course of the exile in the mountains and the exodus to India, in successive stages up to an installation which was at first precarious, the less valiant among them had perished from the toils and hardships, diseases and despair. Thus the small surviving band possessed latent energies only waiting for an opportunity to blossom forth. They can in this respect be compared with the Pilgrims, those English Puritans who, fleeing from religious persecution, went out to found what was to become in two centuries the grandeur that is the United States of America. In the economy, the politics, and the social status of the United States, their descendants still occupy many of the best places. However, the question remains whether the rise of the Parsees—like that of the Puritans—had anything to do with the commandments of their religion.

Here, under the signature of a contemporary Parsee, is a summary of the Mazdean doctrine:[1]

The universe is the creation of Ahura Mazda, the Creator, but it has not come from nothing. The aim of the Creation is the bliss and welfare of man. The sequence of creations differs from that in the Bible: first the sky was created with all the celestial bodies, then water, the earth, the vegetable kingdom and the animal kingdom, and finally man. The duration of creation, from the beginning up to the renovation (*frashokart*) is twelve milleniums. The whole creation is bound by the law of production and destruction. Ahura Mazda's might has two poles, one of which, the Spenta Mainyu, prospers and maintains everything, whereas the other, the Aṅra Mainyu, is the destructive force. Only in the Sassanid period (A.D. 226–631) did the identification of Ahura Mazda, the Creator, with Spenta Mainyu, his maintaining pole, definitively

---

[1] J. M. Unvala, *Wörter und Sachen* (1937), pp. 161 ff.

establish itself; it had already outlined itself in the Videvdat: from then on, Anra Mainyu (Ahriman) acted as counterpart to Ahura Mazda (Ormazd). In this way a certain dualism was formed, but a dualism which did not, as a dualism *stricto sensu* would do, oppose two eternally coexistent deities. Only Ahura Mazda is omnipresent, omniscient, omnipotent, and eternal, whereas Anra Mainyu is limited in time, in power, and in knowledge. His destructive will to power will last up to man's resurrection and the renovation of the world. He will then be annihilated with his bad cohorts, and all evil will be extirpated.

Man is composed of matter and spirit, viz., on the one hand a body, on the other a vital breath, a faculty of discernment, a conscience, a soul and a Fravashi. When the vital breath leaves the body, discernment and conscience perish; only the soul and the Fravashi have a post-mortem existence. Man is born pure, not, as is taught in Christianity, defiled with original sin. To keep his soul from sin, discernment has been given him, a faculty which enables him to distinguish between good and evil and to choose, from free will, either the one or the other. To lead him along the path of righteousness, a Fravashi—comparable, if need be, to Plato's Ideas—is assigned to him. Not only has man's soul a Fravashi, but so has the entire creation, animated or not. The duty of the Fravashi is to see to the prosperity and just growth of the world and to accompany man rightly in his terrestrial life.

Life after death unfolds itself, in the Avestan conception, in Heaven, in Hell, and in an intermediate domain. The decision belongs to the Yazatas Mehr, Sarosh and Rashn, who give their verdict on human deeds. These deeds are the outcome of free will. The actions of children not yet received into the religious community are the entire responsibility of the parents; those of persons under fifteen are half their own, half their parents' responsibility. The Parsee has no concept of fatalism any more than of original sin. Parseeism teaches that we must strive with all our might to obtain the promised bliss and escape the threatening woe. At the end the resurrection of man will take place, which will efface all distinction between good and evil through the latter's annihilation, and will set up an existence in human form, in family groups, exempt from all sin and a source of eternal bliss. All increase of mankind will be ruled out; whence it appears that the doctrines of rebirth and metempsychosis are foreign to Parseeism.

It will be noted that the author, in defining his religion, has taken care to oppose it to Christianity (original sin), to Islam (fatalism), and to Hinduism (transmigration). He concludes with a brief ethics:

The soul's sole advocate at the celestial Judgment after death is the good deeds which he has performed on earth. He should therefore live a righteous life here below. The whole moral doctrine of Zoroastrianism can be summarized in three notions: good thoughts, good words, good deeds. They encompass all that religion teaches in the way of virtues, order and purity, truth and righteousness, obedience and humility, compassion and gratitude, love of parents, family, and compatriots, good treatment of subordinates, care for useful animals, as well as activity, zeal, chastity, self-confidence, hospitality, and generosity. The vices, on the contrary, stem from bad thoughts, bad words, bad deeds.

GEOGRAPHICAL AND HISTORICAL SKETCH

Iran today covers only a part of the territory occupied by the Iranians in the course of their history. One should add to it at least Afghanistan, southwestern Pakistan (Baluchistan), Russian Turkestan as far as the Syr Darya River, the Aral and the Caspian Seas, as well as an area in southern Russia as far as the Black Sea.

Iran, shortened from Iran-shahr, means "land of the Aryas." Before invading this country, the Aryas formed a single group with the future occupants of India, who also called themselves

Aryas. This kinship is proved not only by the identity of name, but also and above all by the comparison of the two languages; and it is likewise reflected in their religion.

Where did these Indo-Iranians live, this offshoot of the larger Indo-European nation? They have left no identifiable material trace. It is known only that they entered India from the northwest, for they first occupied the Punjab (the land of the Indus River and its tributaries) before reaching the Ganges and swarming off into the rest of the Indian subcontinent and beyond. As for the invasion of Iran, we have no knowledge of how it took place.

The presence of Aryas, recognizable by the names they bore, is attested in western Asia from the sixteenth century B.C. on, among the Kassites, who held sway over Babylonia at that time, among the Mitanians, who reigned in Upper Mesopotamia, and as far as Palestine, where their names occur on cuneiform tablets dated from 1600 to 1250 B.C. But it cannot be ascertained whether they were closer to the Aryas of India or to those of Iran.

The main dialectal divisions of Iran, which can be observed in historical times, give the outlines of a tribal division. Four regions may be distinguished, each of which played its own part in the history of the whole nation. The east, separated from the west by the great central desert of the Iranian plateau, except for the series of oases south of the Caspian, was the scene of the birth and first expansion of the Zoroastrian religion. It is there that the oldest parts of the Avesta, the sacred book of this religion, were composed. The northwest, that is, south of the Caspian and the Caucasus, was the country of the Medes, whose King Deioces founded the first Iranian empire (Herodotus, I. 96), with Ecbatana for its capital. They are cited for the first time in 835 B.C. in a cuneiform document reporting a campaign of Shalmaneser III, king of Assyria, against them. The Magi, according to Herodotus, were a Median tribe. The southwest, more exactly the part of the plateau lying along the Persian Gulf, was the land of the *Persae*, whose dialect was clearly different from the rest. It is this region alone that deserves the name Persia (today, Fars), which accordingly ought to be reserved for it. In the middle of the sixth century B.C. the Persian king, Cyrus, subdued the Medes, conquered Babylon (thus liberating the Jews), and founded the Achaemenid empire, which was later to threaten Greece and finally succumbed only to Alexander (331 B.C.).

Achaemenids

Cyrus, who reigned from 558 to 530, had for his capital Pasargadae in Persia. His successor, Cambyses (530–522), conquered Egypt.

The religion of the Achaemenid empire is summarily known through the inscriptions which Darius (522–486) and his successors caused to be engraved on the rock of Behistun (on the road from Babylon to Ecbatana) and in their capitals of Persepolis (near modern Shiraz) and Susa (near Shushtar, in ancient Elam or Susiana, due north of the Persian Gulf). They worshipped Ahura Mazda, but do not cite Zarathushtra. The Magi were their clergy.

Xerxes (486–465) prohibited the cult of the *daivas* (the ancient gods; Sanskrit *deva*, "god"). In 482 he destroyed Babylon, which had rebelled, and suppressed the religion of Marduk, which his predecessors had tolerated.

Artaxerxes I, "the long-handed" (465–425), in order to secure the loyalty of Jerusalem against rebellious Egypt, charged Ezra, chief of the Jews who had remained in Babylon, with the task of reorganizing Jerusalem. He charged Nehemiah, whom he appointed governor in 444, with that of rebuilding its walls.

Under Artaxerxes II, called "Mnemon" (405–359), the Iranian cult, thus far without idols, was provided with statues, in imitation of the Greeks: effigies of the goddess Anahita (the Iranian Artemis) were introduced at Babylon, Susa, and Ecbatana, and her cult extended to Persia, Bactriana (eastern Iran) and Sardis (Asia Minor). The royal inscriptions, which had so far cited only Ahura Mazda, now also named Anahita and Mithra.

The fourth and final region of Iran, to the north, was inhabited by nomads, the Sakas or Scythians, who played an episodic role, through their excursions southwards. Their area reached as far as southern Russia, where they were known to the Greeks. Herodotus described their religion and customs.

Arsacids

A century and a half after Alexander's death, western Iran passed under the domination of the Parthians, an Iranian people that had come from southeast of the Caspian. Mithridates I (171–138 B.C.) was the true founder of the Parthian (or Arsacid) empire, which held the Romans in check. Its capital was Ctesiphon, built near Seleucia, not far from the future Baghdad.

The Semitic element is above all important in the Parthian

cities of Mesopotamia, such as Dura-Europos on the Middle Euphrates.

In eastern Iran, the Iranian, Greek, and Indian religions lived side by side without much mingling. This area, superficially Hellenized by Alexander and the Indo-Bactrian kings which succeeded him (of which Menander was the most famous), underwent at that time several invasions. That of the Sakas, north Iranians, left to a part of the country the name Sakastana ("land of the Sakas"), today called Seistan, partly in Afghanistan and partly in Baluchistan. These were succeeded by the Pahlavas, one of whom, Gondopharnes, was known in Christian legend for having welcomed the Apostle Thomas, and also as one of the three Magi (Gaspar) who had gone to prostrate themselves at Bethlehem.

Up till then, the ancient Iranian religion seems submerged under Hellenism. It crops up again under the rule of the Kushans, the greatest of whom was Kanishka. On their coins Greek, Iranian, and Indian gods are represented. Since they also held sway over India, the Iranian religion reaches into that country, and in the same way Buddhism was introduced into eastern Iran (attested, for instance, by the colossal Buddha statues of Bamiyan, near Kabul).

Sassanids

From 226 A.D. onward, the political center of Iran swung back to Persia, under the Sassanids, who reigned until the Muslim conquest. Zoroastrianism, whose history had so far been obscure, now became the empire's official religion. It had to struggle there not only against Christianity but against a more recent religion as well, Manichaeism, preached by Mani.

This was a gnostic synthesis of Jewish, Greek, Mesopotamian, and Iranian elements, characterized by an absolute dualism in which the good god is confronted with an evil demon, who is equally eternal and is responsible for Creation.

Artaxsher, the founder of the Sassanid dynasty, reigned from A.D. 226 to 241. He had for his son and successor the celebrated Shapur (241–272), who humiliated the Roman Emperor Valerian, an exploit commemorated both by reliefs carved in the rock at Naqsh-i-Rustam[2] (near Persepolis, which Alexander had destroyed), above the rock-tombs of the Achaemenid kings, and by an inscription engraved opposite this rock on the base of a monument, the so-called "Ka'ba of Zoroaster," where it was discovered in 1936.

Artaxsher's minister, Karter, caused another inscription to be engraved below the one just mentioned. Both tell us of the beginnings of Sassanid Mazdaism. Karter outlived his master and, under Varhran I (273–276), caused Mani to be accused and imprisoned; Mani died in chains at the age of 60.

The site of Naqsh-i-Rustam was one of the two religious centers in Sassanid Iran; the other was at Shiz in Media, today Taxt-i-Suleiman.[3] The political centers were at Ctesiphon (the ancient Arsacid capital), Susa, and several places in Persia.

Under Ohrmazd II (303–309), the Iranian empire recovered its lost eastern provinces by annexing the northern kingdom of the Kushans.

His successor, Shapur II, had a very long reign (309–379), during which the persecution of Christianity (which had,

---

[2] A popular name, arising from confusion with the legendary hero Rustam.
[3] Another popular attribution, this time to a figure of the Jewish tradition: Solomon.

since Constantine, become the official religion of the Roman empire) took on a political character.

One century later, Kavad (488–531) favored a new religion, Mazdakism, fatalistic and egalitarian. His son Khosrau I (531–578) restored traditional order and consolidated the Mazdean church by defining orthodoxy and giving the Avesta its definitive form. He took or was given the title Anosharvan, "with an immortal soul." On the other hand, the last Greek philosophers from the Athenian Academy, when their school was closed by order of Justinian in A.D. 529, found asylum at the court of Khosrau, at Ctesiphon.

After Khosrau, the Sassanid empire declined until its end half a century later: it opposed only half-heartedly the Muslim expansion, which decisively defeated the armies of the last Sassanid, Yazdakart III, at Qadisiya (Mesopotamia) in 635.

Islam

Theoretically Islam tolerated the old religion, but conversions, by persuasion or by force, were massive.

However, Mazdaism remained a ferment of rebellion and attracted persecution. There were centers of survival, if not of resistance, notably in Fars, the former center of the Achaemenid and Sassanid empires. This area also knew a kind of Zoroastrian revival, marked by the production of works in Pahlavi (the official language of Sassanid Iran).

One of these works, the *Shkand gumanik Vicar* ("Decisive solution of Doubts") is a defence of Mazdaism against Islam, Christianity, Judaism, and Manichaeism. Another, the *Den-*

kart, is an encyclopedia apparently purporting to salvage
from threatening collapse what was essential in the religion.
One finds in it amongst other things a summary of the entire
Avesta still extant at the time.

The collapse did occur—for reasons not quite clear. The
movement of national revival was seized and diverted by
dynasties of Turkish origin, the Ghaznevids (926–1186) and
Seljuks (1037–1300), which found their support in orthodox
Islam against both the Shiite heresy and Zoroastrianism.
Mahmud the Ghaznevid (so called after his capital, Ghazni,
in Afghanistan) entrusted Firdousi with the task of chanting
the past of Iran in a vast epic, the *Shah Nama* ("Book of
Kings"), placed under the invocation of Allah.

Zoroastrianism survived partly in the form of elements
amalgamated into the Muslim religion of Iran. There were
also a few Mazdean works in the Persian language, such as the
thirteenth-century *Zardusht Nama* ("Book of Zoroaster")
in verse. But in autonomous form it subsisted only in small,
isolated areas, such as those of Yazd and Kerman today, to the
east of Persia.

Emigration

One or more groups of Zoroastrians, from the tenth century
onward (so it seems, rather than from the eighth, as generally
believed), made for the Persian Gulf, then for India, where
they found asylum in Gujarat. Contact appears to have been
almost completely severed up to the end of the fifteenth century. Renewed in 1477, it was maintained notably in the form
of an exchange of letters until 1768. These letters, seventeen
of which have been preserved, are the Rivayats. They contain

the questions and answers exchanged between the Parsees of India and their cousins in Iran on matters of law, ritual, etc.

In the sixteenth century Emperor Akbar attempted to found a syncretistic religion, chiefly based on Zoroastrianism and Islam. In the seventeenth century, under Akbar's grandson, Zoroastrian mystics who had come from Persia inspired a work, the *Dabistan,* which is vaguely universalistic and largely allegorizing. In the eighteenth century, Parseeism was divided into two sects on a question of calendar and ritual, following contacts with the old tradition preserved in Iran. At the same time the holders of this tradition endeavored to instruct their coreligionists in India; these were able in turn to explain the Avesta to the Frenchman Anquetil-Duperron, who translated it in 1771. It was then that the investigation of the Mazdean traditions by European scholars began, which made its greatest progress since the *Commentaire sur le Yasna,* a commentary on part of the Avesta published by Burnouf in 1833, and has in turn helped the Parsees to rediscover their religious past.

Accused of dualism by the Christian missionaries, the Parsees tend to minimize this aspect of their religion. They were greatly helped in this by the German scholar Haug in a lecture given at Poona in 1861, as well as by his other works and those of his successors, which bring Zoroaster's monotheism to the fore.

This return of an elite to its religious origins brought about a division into reformists and reactionaries. The division concerned notably the value of prayers and ceremonies for the dead.

Despite the attempts at purgation, Parseeism remained

encumbered with adventitious elements. Astrology is current in it. Theosophic doctrines have crept in.

The Parsees of India have done much to help their poor brothers in Iran (whom the Muslims call *Gabars*, "infidels") and to secure a better social status for them from the Iranian government.

Since India became independent in 1947, the status of the Parsees has been threatened and diminished by a regime which, tending towards a form of socialism or state capitalism, attacks the private fortunes. Since nothing can henceforward subsist without state help, the Parsee schools, for instance, will have to open their doors to non-Parsees—or perish. What will presently be left of their beliefs and customs, of the very consciousness that they form a group, and of their will to maintain it? It is conceivable that the Parsee community may vanish into the melting pot of the new India. The smallest of the great religions would then cease to exist.

I
Forms of Symbolization

The Parsees give their customs and beliefs a symbolical meaning. In this they do not differ from the adepts of other religions; for it can be said that religious reflection, always and everywhere, largely consists in wondering about the reason and the purpose of a particular rite. Afterwards—and perhaps only beyond a certain level of naïveté—is this wonder directed to the hidden sense of a particular myth.

No religion can totally free itself from ritual. Even in the most spiritualized ones, for instance, some forms of Protestantism, there crops up now and then a certain nostalgia for ritual. Men have ceased to believe in the intrinsic, quasi-magical value of gestures and objects. These are discarded as magic, as idolatry; but they are preserved as symbols. "From magic to symbol": such could be the formula of a normal religious evolution. In the less spiritualized forms, religion has stopped somewhere halfway, at a stage which, to use Saint Augustine's term, may be called sacramental.

The interpretation of a rite is often a matter of uncertainty, hence of variation and renewal. This is no evidence of weakness. Indeed, could it not be said that a living religion is one that reinterprets its practices? Thus, according to the *Dabistan,* the apocryphal Iranian work of the seventeenth century, the sound of the mortar struck with the pestle in order to avert evil spirits becomes, on a second level of symbolism, a reminder of the thoughts, words, and deeds which will intervene at the coming of the future Saviors.

In most cases the visible, material action is representative of an invisible, spiritual one. But sometimes it simply represents, by a kind of euphemism, another reality. We see the difficulty of explaining symbols without resorting to other symbols when we read what J. J. Modi, a Parsee scholar, has to say of the *kunkun*:

The red pigment mark on the forehead of a bride is always round and that on the forehead of a bridegroom always long and vertical. The reason is this: the long vertical mark of the male symbolizes a ray of the sun, and the round mark of the female symbolizes the moon. A handsome man is compared by oriental writers with the sun, but the beauty of a woman is always compared with that of the moon. The sun is always represented in ancient pictures as a round disc with shooting rays. Again, the sun, through its rays, is a fructifying agent, but the moon is represented as a conceiving agent. She absorbs the rays of the sun. Just as the sun is a fructifying agent, and the moon a conceiving agent, so is man in his relation to woman. Hence it is that the mark on a man's forehead is long and vertical like the rays of the sun, and that on a woman's forehead round like the moon.[1]

What a roundabout way of telling us that these dots and bars are sexual symbols!

To avoid being arbitrary, any study of religious symbolism will have to proceed in a historical, comparative fash-

---

[1] *The Religious Ceremonies and Customs of the Parsees* (Bombay, 1937), p. 22.

ion. For instance, the façade of a rock-tomb (probably Median) at Kizkapan shows two men, undoubtedly Magi, on either side of a fire altar across which they face each other. They are wearing caps which cover their mouth, their left hands rest on their bows while their right are lifted in front of them, with the palm held vertically. The same attitude is found on the monumental façade of the rock-tomb of Darius at Naqsh-i-Rustam, (see Fig. 1): on a huge throne carried by slaves stands Darius, facing a burning altar, under the winged disk representing the sky god, with, behind it, a full disk whose under edge is swollen in the shape of a crescent, a probable figuration of the sun and the moon. The king holds in his left hand his bow, resting on the ground, while his right hand makes the gesture we have just described: a gesture of prayer, designated in the Gathas by the term *ustana-zasta,* "with outstretched hand." The same gesture is attributed to the god, as can be seen on the relief dominating the great inscription which Darius ordered to be engraved on the rock of Behistun: Ahura Mazda, emerging from the winged disk (an old Egyptian symbol whose history will be recalled further on), holds in his left hand the Ring of Power, whilst he raises his right hand with the palm held vertically. The identity of the gesture is enough to establish a link between the faithful one and his god.

In the beliefs, the domain of symbolism tends to expand as critical reflection develops, for they can no more be accepted literally. The Parsees have gone very far in this direction: ever since the Middle Ages, Ahriman, their Devil, has occasionally been interpreted away as "the evil tendencies in Man." This allegorizing can end in the complete dissipation of a myth. In a catechism published by Modi in 1911, one would look in vain for the slightest trace of Ahriman.

In our Western civilization the method of allegorical interpretation has been in use since early antiquity, but it always had adversaries who warned against its excesses. It was first applied to Homer and Hesiod by Theagenes of Rhegium as early as the sixth century B.C. He insisted that the battle of the gods was an allegory of a moral conflict; the judgment of Paris signified a debate between faculties of the soul. In this way, old myths were saved in the minds of a more critical age.

Sometimes the method was a means of masking unorthodox ideas under the appearance of tradition. Thus, according to Stoic materialism, the gods represented the elements, Hera the air, etc. Philo the Jew and others applied the classical method of allegorical interpretation to the Old Testament: anthropomorphic statements about God were not to be taken literally but as allegories, etc. Paul inaugurated the "typology" of the Old Testament, which consists in finding in every feature of the ancient Scriptures a prefiguration of some event of the new era. Origen carried on what Philo and Paul had begun. Today a thinker like Bultmann, with his "demythologizing," reflects essentially the same attitude.

This tendency had, as we said, its detractors in the Occident. For several reasons, one of them being for the sake of reason itself, it was combated by Xenophanes, Heraclitus, and Plato, by Epicurus and the New Academy, by the grammarians of Alexandria and by Emperor Julian, and by many Christians, including Arnobius. But in the Middle Ages this opposition ceased.

The preoccupation with symbols was renewed in the Romantic period in the context of the medieval revival; then in the symbolist movement, in Freudianism and Jungianism, and finally in surrealism: all these movements were characterized by an obsession with symbols.

In Parseeism there was never an explicit resistance to allegorism, and one of its modern high priests, Dastur Khurshed S. Dabu, writes in his *Message of Zarathushtra* (Bombay 1956) that almost every belief is symbolic. For instance: "Some portions of the Avesta, if taken literally, would seem absurd. Mountains, rivers and similar topographical features do not refer to any physical locations, but probably to some psycho-physiological features, some psychic currents within the human body (brain, nerves or some plexus or gland, etc.). . . ."

Such an exaggeration is conducive of mistrust. But one should be careful not to go to the other extreme and pretend that all allegorical interpretations are adventitious. To remain objective the historian of religion will first seek the texts where the use of allegory is explicit and avowed.

THE SOUL AND THE MAIDEN

When the soul of a departed, after three days, leaves the body on the fourth dawn, the young girl who appears to him "beautiful, radiant, white-armed, robust, fair-faced, erect, high-breasted, of stately form, noble-born, of glorious lineage, fifteen years old in appearance, as beautiful in form as the most beautiful of creatures" is explicitly "his own conscience": "What damsel art thou, the most beautiful of damsels in form which I have ever seen?" "O thou youth of Good Thought, Good Word, Good Deed, Good Conscience, I am the Conscience of thine own self." And she adds: "So me, being lovable, thou madest still more lovable; me, being beautiful, thou madest still more beautiful; me, being desirable, thou madest still more desirable; me, sitting in a high place, thou madest sitting in a still higher place." The wicked one, on the contrary, meets a hag who speaks to him in the opposite fashion: like Dorian Gray, he is faced with the picture of his moral ugliness.

We can follow the complete history of this transparent allegory, from its Indo-Iranian origins up to its ultimate adoption by Islam. Comparison with India allows us to grasp it in its nascent state. A pre-allegorical state is implied by the Indian myth according to which the soul is welcomed by Apsarases (female beings similar to Islam's houris), who come to meet it with fruit, unguents, crowns, garments, and fragrant powder. They adorn him like Brahma himself. (We shall come back to the important motif of the soul's garments, a motif which is probably the origin of the "glorious bodies" of resurrection mentioned by Saint Paul.) What is interesting in the present context is the fact that two of the Apsarases have abstract names: Manasi and Cakshushi, "the intelligent one" and "the seeing one," which means that they incarnate and symbolize two faculties which the soul will need in its new state—or two virtues which it has displayed. The celestial harem has already undergone a partial transformation in the direction of abstraction, if not of ethics— a process which was to end in Iran with the clear allegory of Damsel-Conscience.

In Islam, besides the primitive belief in houris (who are heavenly courtesans like the Apsarases), an obvious borrowing from Iran is found in the belief that the departed soul meets the personification of its actions, either a bright, beautiful, perfumed figure if they have been good, or a horrible, dark, and foul-smelling one if they were bad. But instead of the female sex it has in Mazdeism, most commentators make this figure masculine. This is in accordance with Muslim aesthetics, which gives as the prototype of human beauty not a woman but a man, namely Joseph.

MULTIFARIOUSNESS OF THE SYMBOLS

The *kusti,* or girdle, is the obligatory emblem of every Mazdean, who ties and unties it several times a day. A multiple symbolism is attached to it, as will be seen in the next chapter. In the universe its counterpart is the Milky Way. On the other hand, the girdle which Ahura Mazda offered to Haoma (the sacred liquor) symbolizes "the good Mazdean religion," and this symbolism is expressed, in Yasna 9 of the Avesta, by a direct apposition: "To thee, Haoma, Ahura Mazda brought a girdle, the good Mazdean religion." The same identification is found in a Pahlavi text of Zatspram, IV, 4–6 (tr. Zaehner, *Zurvan,* p. 163): "The Religion was manifested in Spandarmat at the time when Frasyab withheld the waters from Iran and Spandarmat brought them back. . . . She was arrayed in a bright robe which shone forth in all directions for a *hasr's* length, that is, about two *parasangs.* And she was girt with a golden girdle which was the Religion of the Mazdayasnians." It would be impossible to state the symbolic relationship between two terms more strongly.

Ohrmazd's throne represents the god himself in the vision, described in the *Datastan i Denik* (eighteenth question), of the souls of the good and the wicked (sic). Here is how this relationship is expressed: "The souls of the righteous and

wicked see in the spiritual places the throne, which they deem
a sign of Ohrmazd."

Elsewhere, the symbolic interpretation is offered as the
explanation of a dream: for instance in the narrative of
Zoroaster's visions at the beginning of the Vohuman Yasn or
Bahman Yasht:

Ohrmazd showed the wisdom of all-knowledge unto Zaratuxsht.
Through it, he saw the trunk of a tree, on which there were four
branches: one of gold, one of silver, one of steel, and one of mixed
iron . . . When he arose from sleep, he, Zaratuxsht, spoke: Lord
of the spiritual and material existences! It seems that I saw the
trunk of a tree, on which there were four branches. He, Ohrmazd,
spoke to Spitaman Zaratuxsht: The trunk of a tree, which thou
sawest, is the material existence, which I, Ohrmazd, created. The
four branches are the four periods which will come. That of gold
is that when I and thou will hold a conference, King Vishtasp
shall accept the religion, the figures of the *divs* shall totter, and
they will remain from publicity into distant and concealed movements. That of silver is the reign of Artaxsher the Kai. And that
of steel is the reign of Khosrau, son of Kavat, of immortal soul.
And that of mixed iron is the evil sovereignty of the *divs*, having
dishevelled hair, the seed of Aeshma, when thy tenth century will
be at an end, O Spitaman Zaratuxsht!"

Then the prophet has another dream, in the course of
which he sees a tree with seven branches, the meaning of
which is explained as before. In this second vision, the old
myth of the ages of the world, also known to Hesiod and in
India, has undergone a change which seems attributable to
the influence of astrological beliefs, the number seven corresponding to that of the planets. Such a pattern seems at the
origin of the seven-door ladder mentioned by Celsus in a
passage quoted by his great adversary Origen: "One finds in
the doctrine of the Persians and in the cult of Mithras a sym-

bol of the two revolutions of the sky, that of the fixed stars and that of the planets, and of the passage of the souls through the latter. This symbol consists in this: a ladder with seven doors and above it an eighth one."[2] The first door is of lead and consecrated to Saturn (the softest metal to the slowest planet); the second one, of brass, to Venus; and so on up to the sun, in an order which is exactly the opposite of that of the days in the week.

Why this order? Why does the soul, arising from the earth, not cross the planetary circles in the order of their increasing distance, i.e.: Moon, Mercury, Venus, Sun, Mars, Jupiter, and Saturn? In order to solve this difficulty one has to surmise, with Cumont,[3] that this ladder was not primarily what Celsus tells us it was, but a figuration of the ages of mankind and of the world, comparable to that in the second vision of the Vohuman Yasn. But why the opposite order to the days of the week? Because, beginning with the age of Saturn, the golden age of mankind, one wished to end with that of the Sun, i.e., of the Savior (as taught in the Oracle of Hystaspes), and to put the age of the worst evils, that of the Moon, in the last place but one. In order to do that it was sufficient to take the week backwards. After the reign of the Sun, a new golden age to which Virgil alludes,[4] there came as the last age that of eternal heaven or infinite time, corresponding to the fixed stars and represented by the eighth door above Celsus' ladder. A picture of this ladder has been found in mosaic in one of the mithraea at Ostia.

In one case the symbol and its significance are presented

[2] *Contra Celsum,* 6.22.
[3] "La Fin du monde selon les mages occidentaux," *Revue d'Histoire des Religions* (1931), pp. 46 ff.
[4] *Toto surget gens aurea mundo . . . iam regnat Apollo (Eclogues,* 4. 4–10.)

dramatically: in the *Karnamak i Artaxsher i Papakan*, which tells of the seizure of power by Artaxsher, the founder of the Sassanid dynasty. Artaxsher was a page at the court of Artaban, the Arsacid emperor. One night, thanks to the complicity of a maidservant who loved him, he succeeded in running away with her on horseback, in order to escape the king's jealousy. On the day after, the king and an escort set out to pursue them, and questioned peasants along the way. The first answer they got is that two people on horseback have been seen, followed closely by a ram. Further on, they were told that two people on a horse were seen, with a ram riding behind. The king questioned the Magi and astrologers in his escort, who explained to him that the game was up: this ram represented the royal destiny. If it had caught up with the fugitives, it meant that Artaxsher was destined to reign.

This royal destiny, or Xvarenah (in Pahlavi, *xvarr*), is habitually represented in another way, by a halo or "glory," and in fact, the Aramaic ideogram which designates it in the Pahlavi texts is the word *gadā*, "glory, brightness."[5] We shall find representations of it on coins. But, apart from all figuration or concrete representation, the fact itself of conceiving and designating Fortune, royal or otherwise, depends on the capacity for symbolizing.

The heroes of yore were supposed to have handed down to each other not only the sacred word (*vaxsh*), but also a *Xvarr*, a Fortune or Dignity. This was not a royal privilege, for Mashya and Mashyane, the first human couple, had theirs, and Zarathushtra had his. It is said of Mashya and Mashyane in *Bundahishn* 14.2 that when they were still united and merged in a rhubarb stem, their *Xvarr* hovered above them

---

[5] Cf. below, Ch. IV.

and it was the *Xvarr* of men. It is therefore the "human form," a principle which was to give them that human appearance which they still lacked. A little further on *xvarr* is glossed by *xveshkarih* ("own function"), then by *ruvan* ("soul").

Certain notions were more or less personified. One recalls at once the Entities, so characteristic of Zoroaster's system, although most of them were probably anterior to him. Prior to him also, and at least as early as the Indo-Iranian period, Iran was familiar with a god who is a personified notion: Mithra, whose name means "Contract"; and it probably also knew of the divinization of Time, "Zurvan." We shall study the Entities, Mithra, and Zurvan in that order.

THE ENTITIES

The Entities which in Zoroaster's system form Ahura Mazda's escort already had a long past, several of them going back to the Indo-Iranian period. This is certainly the case with Asha (Vedic: Rta) and Armaiti (Vedic: Aramati). Most of the others probably existed as notions in the Indo-Iranian period but were still only partly personified.

Asha

It has been denied that Rta was personified in the Veda. This is a question of terms. Rta is not represented in human form, but it is nevertheless referred to as a person, since one hymn (Rig Veda I.75.5) states that Agni should worship not only Mitra-Varuna and the other gods but also the lofty Rta, while another passage calls to help, amongst other gods, "the great Rta" (X.66.4).

The high antiquity of that personification is indeed warranted by the proper names of Aryan chiefs of Mitani, Syria, and Palestine containing this term: Artamanya, Artasumara, Artadama, Artamna. This tradition was continued in historical Iran, notably with the Median kings: the cuneiform texts yield, under Salmanassar III (858–824 B.C.), an Artasari; under his successor, an Artasariru. In Persian times we have King Artaxerxes, or more exactly, Artaxshathra.

What did *asha-rta* mean? Ever since the authors of the Petersburg Dictionary, whose opinion was taken over notably by Bergaigne and Oldenberg, it has been customary to see in the *rta* not only truth (*rtam vad* means "to tell the truth") but the order of things, be it in nature, or in the liturgy, or in moral conduct. It could be inferred that the Indo-Iranians had conceived of a sort of great cosmic law, controlling both the course of the heavenly bodies and the behavior of men.

Against this interpretation Lüders protested in 1910,[6] but the full details of his demonstration were only published posthumously.[7] The gist of it is that the Vedic authors did not have the notion of a universal order. *Rta* is merely the truth, the non-lie, and if it influences the course of the stars and human conduct, ritual or otherwise, it is in virtue of the magical power of the true utterance, of the exact formula uttered in the cult. The ceremony which brings this power into play is well known, although its name is not attested in Sanskrit: it is the *saccakiriya* of the Pali texts. In order to obtain the favor of a god, one pronounces a truth (not necessarily a reminder of a former favor of this god), and this secures success.

[6] *Sitzungsberichte Preuss. Akad. Wiss.* (1910), p. 931.
[7] H. Lüders, *Varuna*, 2 vols. in continuous pagination (1951–1960).

This new thesis soon had supporters, and as early as 1911 Andreas and Wackernagel applied it to the Gathas, translating *asha* as "truth." They are still followed today by Gershevitch, Humbach, Thieme, etc. However, the new thesis of Lüders was rejected by Oldenberg in 1915 in favor of the former one, and by Bernhard Geiger in 1916 and 1934.[8] These authors have, among other things, drawn our attention to the impossibility in certain passages to take *anrta* as "non-truth." The clearest of these passages is Rig Veda VIII.86.6, where a sinner, addressing himself to Varuna, begs forgiveness for his unconscious faults: "It was not intentional, it was a blindness, drink, anger, the dice; and even sleep does not avert *anrta.*" The obvious sense of the last word is undoubtedly "fault," "sin," "non-observance of the law."

Lüders, who boasts of taking all the passages into account (contrary to his predecessors), does not take up this one in the detailed demonstration he gives in pages 402 to 654 of his book. He quotes it only in the introductory summary (p. 36), where he obstinately translates *anrta* by "lie," although the whole context, as he himself admits, speaks of fault and of sin. Nevertheless Lüders' analyses have had a positive result by showing the magic origin of the cosmic value given the *rta.* (For, while maintaining the translation "truth," he speaks of it as a "cosmic force," a "magic potency.") But he thought he had discovered within the Veda this process by which a mere utterance from the mouth of men becomes a force in the universe. It is more difficult to follow him here, for we do not witness this process developing in the Veda. We

---

[8] Oldenberg, *Nachricht der Götting. Gelehr. Gesellsch.* (1915), pp. 167 ff.; Geiger, *Die Amesha Spentas* (1916), *"Rta und Verwandtes,"* *Wiener Zeitschr. f. d. Kunde d. Morgenl.* (1934), pp. 107 ff.

see at once the result of it, the conception of the *rta* as a cosmic and moral power. This conception is not only Vedic, but is found also, as we shall see presently, in Iran.

The *rta* materializes itself in light, as is shown by Lüders himself (p. 619). Similarly in Iran, according to Zoroaster (Yasna 31.7), Asha filled the space with lights.

Avestan *ashavan* ("follower of Asha") must very soon have come to mean "just," "good" (in contradistinction to *dregvant*, "follower of the Druj"), a meaning which is that of Pahlavi *ahrav*. However, since it could be objected that this is a purely Iranian development, or even a purely Zoroastrian one, it is best left out of account; we can then consider only the Old Persian term *artavan*. This connotes a quality of the deceased ("and may I, dead, be *artava*," says Xerxes, in *Persepolis* 48), which corresponds perfectly—as shown recently by Kuiper[9]—to Vedic *rtavan*, an epithet of gods, of the deceased fathers, and of death, the essential point being that *rta* is linked up with the domain of death: "it is regularly hidden where the sun's horses are unharnessed" (Rig Veda V.62.1).

On the whole, the conception of *rta* objectified as a cosmic power proves to be of Indo-Iranian date. It matters little, then, whether we persist in translating it by "truth," which recalls its far-off genesis, or whether on the contrary we prefer not to overburden the word "truth" with implications it hardly has in our languages and to stick more closely to the Vedic term's definition, formulated by Geiger as follows: "the Right (including the idea of truth) as a cosmic force, the norm for decent behavior, the guide for all actions."

[9] *Indo-Iranian Journal* (1959), p. 215.

Armaiti

One can hardly doubt that Armaiti and Vedic Aramati were one and the same person, in spite of Bailey's attempt to separate them.[10] Aramati is indeed a person: Rig Veda V.43.6 invokes her as "the great consenting Aramati, the divine woman." On the other hand, if Sayana's gloss identifying her with the Earth is in itself worthless, it tallies with the unanimous evidence of the Iranian texts which associate Armaiti with the earth, from Yasna 42.3, in which "the Spirit created, for the cow's pasture, Aramaiti," up to the earth's "patronage" by Spandarmat in the Pahlavi works; thus one can conclude, for instance with Wesendonk,[11] that there existed already in Indo-Iranian times a goddess Aramati of Piety, Devotion, etc. (according to her name's etymology: "agreeing thought"), but also of the Earth.

The other entities do not appear as persons. However the antiquity of their personification is demonstrable, as far as two of them are concerned, in an indirect fashion.

Haurvatat and Ameretat

In the Avesta these two Entities are patrons of the waters and plants, and already one Gatha (Yasna 51.7) significantly parallels both couples: "O thou who hast fashioned the cow and the waters and the plants, give me Immortality and Integrity." Now, as shown by Darmesteter,[12] the idea that the

[10] *Bulletin of the School Oriental Studies* (1935), p. 142.
[11] "Aramati als arische Erdgottheit," *Archiv f. Religionswiss.* (1929), pp. 61 ff.
[12] *Haurvatat and Ameretat* (1875).

waters and plants are apt to procure health and to rescue from death goes back to the Indo-Iranian period. But moreover, there are, between the Indian myths of the Ashvins and the Muslim legends of Harut and Marut (medieval forms of our two entities) traits of similarity too precise to be attributable to chance.[18] One must conclude that if not with the Indo-Iranians, at least in Iran before Nanhaithya's downfall to the rank of a demon, Haurvatat and Ameretat were conceived as persons, as subjects of myths.

Another Entity, Xshathra, if not personified, is at least attributable to the Indo-Iranian period with a characteristic value.

Xshathra

In the Veda, *ksatra* has its primary sense of "power, might"; its derivate only means "sovereign." But one passage (VIII. 35.17) already shows the specialization which in classical Sanskrit will cause *ksatriya* to designate the warrior class: whereas stanzas 16 and 18 say, respectively, "favor the *brahman* and the prayers" and "favor the cows and the *vishah*," the intermediate stanza has this: "favor the *ksatra* and the warrior." It could be thought that this development was late and peculiar to India. But the name of one of the Nart family, in the Ossetic legend, namely the Æxsærtægkatæ, who distinguish themselves by their bravery, allows us to go back to Indo-Iranian.

Dubious for the Indo-Iranian period is the existence of two Entities not yet considered here, Vohu Manah and Spenta Mainyu.

[18] G. Dumézil, *Naissance d' archanges* (1945), ch. V.

Vohu Manah

Vedic *manas* lacks the epithet "good" which would make it parallel to *vohu manah*. In order to find in Vedic a more exact correspondent to the Iranian term, as far as the meaning is concerned, one must consider with Geiger,[14] the word *sumati*. This word, from the same root as *manas-manah,* is admittedly specialized, for it designates more precisely benevolence (in gods), and prayer (in men). But this results from a secondary evolution, and Geiger does not hesitate to conclude that "the concept of good thought had already attained personification in the Indo-Iranian period."

Spenta Mainyu

In Vedic *manyu* means "impetuosity," "ardor," "spirit," etc. Thus in Rig Veda I.139.2 Mitra and Varuna keep disorder away from order "by the liveliness (*manyuna*) of their will." A whole hymn, studied by Güntert,[15] is addressed to Manyu personified. Manyu is the psychic force, a divine force which gives triumph in battle, etc.

The meaning of *mainyu* in the Avesta cannot be reduced to this Vedic notion. Perhaps the Zoroastrian tendency affected this term so far as to cut it off from its origins.

The Order of the Entities

A question presents itself about the Entities, either considered in themselves or as Ahura Mazda's escort: why those

[14] *Die Amesha Spentas,* p. 241.
[15] *Der Arische Weltkönig und Heiland* (1925), pp. 104 ff.

and not others? Is there a principle to their choice? In order
to answer this question, their order should be studied. Indeed,
when they are enumerated, it is not in an indifferent order
but in a list which, apart from certain variations easily accounted for, is remarkably fixed. Here is this list, as it results
notably from Bundahishn, chapter I. Let us note before-
hand that the place of Spenta Mainyu, the first one, has been
taken over by Ohrmazd himself, with whom that Spirit had
long been identified: Ohrmazd, Vohu Manah, Asha, Xshathra,
Haurvatat, and Ameretat.

According to Gershevitch,[16] this order is justified by that
of the "elements" and other material objects patronized by
these Entities, i.e.: man, the ox, fire, metals, the earth, waters
and plants. The list of Entities would represent or imply a
certain analysis of the universe.

This explanation is not convincing, for such a heteroclite
succession of elements in which fire and the metals are inter-
calated between the ox and the earth and from which the
wind is absent would itself require justification. If, however,
one accepts this strange analysis of the physical world, will it
be made the basis of the system of Entities by deriving each
of these from the element of which it is patron? This has been
attempted, without success, by L. H. Gray in his article "The
double nature of the Iranian Archangels."[17] Generally speaking, the mere fact that the Entities wear abstract names pre-
cludes any attempt to find a concrete origin for them.[18]

Another principle is therefore required for the list of entities. Now, this principle becomes apparent as soon as one

---

[16] *The Avestan Hymn to Mithra* (1959), pp. 9 ff.

[17] *Archiv f. Religionswiss.* (1904), pp. 349 ff.

[18] For instance, Nyberg's attempt in his *Religionen des alten Iran* (1938)
to see in them the sublimation of collectivities.

takes the fact into account, following Dumézil, that this list
is parallel to that of the social functions and of the gods
which represent them. This parallelism is not fortuitous, for
each entity has, with its opposite god, a particular affinity,
demonstrable by other means. We may summarize what
Georges Dumézil has expounded at length.[19]

Vohu Manah protects the cattle, as Mithra is the god "with
wide pastures"; Asha is identical to Vedic Rta, which is
guarded by Varuna. In the same way Xshathra corresponds
to the *ksatra,* patronized by Indra. Haurvatat and Ameretat
were closely associated, as we have seen, to the Iranian opposite numbers of the two Nasatyas. If we provisionally neglect
Ohrmazd and Armaiti, we obtain a list of entities exactly
parallel to that of the gods of Mitani:

Vohu Manah	Mitra
Asha	Varuna
Xshathra	Indra
Haurvatat/Ameretat	the two Nasatyas

The list enumerates, in their order, the three social functions: Sovereignty (under its two aspects), War, Fecundity.

We have yet to justify the places of Armaiti and Ohrmazd
and to mention a variation of order between Vohu Manah
and Asha.

Armaiti, who was trivalent, could be put on any rank; but
her homologue Anahita being above all a goddess of fecundity
and more important than the Nasatyas, it seemed proper to
place her immediately before them. As for Ohrmazd, or
previously Spenta Mainyu, it was natural that he should come

[19] *Naissance d'Archanges* (1945); *Les Dieux des Indo-Européens* (1953);
L'idéologie tripartie des Indo-Européens (1958).

first, as the great god or creator. It is not necessary to invoke an affinity, in itself probable, between Spenta Mainyu (Anra Mainyu's twin) and Vayu's "good" half (twin to the bad half of this god) or to recall Vayu-Janus' "initial" character, beside his warlike character. It should be observed, however, that if Vayu did once belong to the list, the element wind, which he patronized, figured accordingly in the list of physical things, where its absence surprises us. On the presence of Man at the beginning of the Pahlavi list we shall have to speak again in chapter four.

The rank of Vohu Manah and Asha is subject to variation, as we have said. Indeed, three Gatha texts (Yasna 27.15, 37.4, and 35) tell us that the first and greatest Amesha Spenta is Asha. Everywhere else Vohu Manah comes first. Asha's priority is in accord with Varuna's, whereas that of Vohu Manah reproduces Mitra's anteriority in the compound *mitravaruna*, an anteriority due merely to the linguistic rule which states that in a *dvandva* the shorter term comes first. In this way the list of Amesha Spentas seems to reflect even in this variation the divine hierarchy and its linguistic expression.

The tripartite ideology allows us to elucidate completely the series of material objects patronized by the Entities. For some of them, the connection is self-evident: the earth and the waters and plants are quasi-identical with Armaiti, Haurvatat and Ameretat; fire is associated to Asha, as it is in the Veda, as sacrificial fire, since Rta-Asha is the norm of liturgy. One reads in Rig Veda V.12.6: "Whoever, O Agni, honors thy sacrifice with veneration, that one guards the *rta*." Similarly in the Gathas, it is with sacrificial fire that Asha is associated.

For the ox and the metals the connection is not obvious;

here the tripartite ideology gives the clue. Vohu Manah patronized the ox as Mithra is master of wide pastures. Xshathra, the Entity of the war function, patronizes the metals, of which weapons are made.

Zoroaster's System

One can now see in what Zoroaster's intervention consisted. Having at his disposition a double traditional system of gods and Entities, he did not substitute the latter for the former: had a substitution taken place, one cannot see why Varuna (or the Ahura, to speak Iranian) should have had two substitutes, Asha in the list, Ahura Mazda above it; in other words, if Asha replaced ancient Ahura, why was there still need of Ahura Mazda?

Provided with this double list, Zoroaster struck out all the gods save one: he ignored Mithra and condemned all the others, who were mere *daevas;* but he allowed all the Entities to survive by annexing or subordinating them to Ahura Mazda. This annexation was made chiefly through "filiation." We read in the Gathas—and this is why, no doubt, Strabo could say that the Magi, when sacrificing, recited a theogony[20] —that Ahura Mazda is the father of Spenta Mainyu, Asha, Vohu Manah, and Armaiti; whereas the three inferior Entities, Xshathra, Haurvatat, and Ameretat, are only said to be his, to be in his possession. This does not mean that he is not also their father; both ways of speaking occur in the case of Armaiti (in Yasna 45.4 and 31.9 respectively). And according to a more recent text Ashi is called the daughter of Ahura

[20] Schaeder, *Zeitschr, der deutschen Morgenl. Gesellsch.* (1940), p. 404.

Mazda and the sister of the Amesha Spentas, who are therefore all of them his children.

Ashi is, with Sraosha, an entity about which we have said nothing yet, as these two were not part of the system, although in the Pahlavi works Sraosha was added to it. The list was not closed, and even Varhran, albeit not an entity, was later added to it also.[21]

Sraosha

The entity Sraosha, "Discipline," corresponded, as Dumézil has shown, to the ancient god Airyaman, whom Zoroaster ignored as he did Mithra, and who was a sort of satellite of Mitra, devoted to the protection of persons. When Mithra, in the later Avesta, came to be honored again, Sraosha was his acolyte, with Rashnu: all three sit as judges at the entrance to the hereafter, doubtless because of the "intermediary" role (in this case, between this world and the other) of Mithra, the *mesites* mentioned by Plutarch.

Ashi

This entity, whose name means "Retribution," "windfall," and who has been extensively studied by Wolfgang Schulze,[22] has been recognized as corresponding to Indian Bhaga, who is a satellite of Mitra devoted to the distribution of riches. Provided with the epithet *vanuhi* ("good"), Ashi was very

[21] J. de Menasce, "La Promotion de Varhram," *Revue de l'hist. des religions*, 133 (1947), pp. 5 ff.
[22] *Oriental Studies in honour of . . . Pavry* (1932), pp. 407 ff.

much favored, along with Mithra and others, in the Bactriana of the Kushans.

Ahura Mazda and the Entities

Zoroaster had other means of expressing Ahura Mazda's sovereignty besides calling him Father or Possessor of the Entities. Ahura Mazda assumes in himself all sovereignty, all "ahurity." However, one still says "the ahuras" (Yasna 30.9) to designate, together with him, Ashi, Sraosha, Rashnu, the Amesha Spentas: all Entities.

Zoroaster's poems are manifestly a meditation on the Entities, and it seems that the prophet's original experience and the subject of his day-to-day mental life consisted in thinking them over, in insistently formulating their relationship with the supreme god. The initial illumination, which was to lighten up for him all this spiritual itinerary, might well have been the one chanted in *Yasna* 43 and which according to tradition he underwent at the age of thirty. Like Isaiah exclaiming "Holy, holy, holy is the Lord . . . ," he chants, "I acknowledge Thee as holy beneficent, O Wise Lord. . . ." And the ray of light spreads itself. Holy beneficent is also one of the two primeval Spirits; holy beneficent will be Armaiti.

Another epithet, *vohu* ("good") is also applied to several Entities; that half of the *manah* which takes sides with the Beneficent Spirit is said to be *vohu:* Vohu Manah is the name under which the "human, mithraic" aspect of the heavenly sovereignty will survive. Vohu Manah is a kind of Providence, God turning toward man, revealing himself to him and helping him. And it is also, on the other hand, the human virtue of "good thought." The epithet is affixed to the Xshathra "Empire or Dominion," Indra's former appanage, which becomes Ahura Mazda's Good Dominion. The same adjective again, in the superlative, extolls Asha, henceforth "the Best Order," Asha vahishta. It is the ideal law, the divine plan—Varuna's previous domain—the standard of all human action but, unlike Vohu Manah, far from all contact with man.

A last qualification, *vairya* ("desirable," "to be chosen"), transmutes the meaning of Xshathra "Dominion" and projects it into an eschatological perspective. This Good Dominion is a kingdom to come, which is announced and for which one must take sides. It will be the reward of the just.

In this way, through the revelation of novel epithets, Ahura Mazda's escort is organized over against the forces of evil. Thanks to Ahura Mazda and his "family" of Entities, thanks especially to the doctrine of the twin Spirits and the choice they make, Zoroaster propounded a monotheistic solution to the old Asha-Druj dualism. His god is creator of light and darkness and master of time.

The doctrine of the Entities also allows Zoroaster to put every faithful one in communion with the supreme god, since they are at once divine and human. Since the "divine" sense is the clearer and the more frequent one, it will suffice to cite here some of the rarer cases where the "human" sense is at least predominant: "I who desire, O Wise Lord, to approach you with good thought" (28.2): "the one (Zarathushtra) who upholds Order" (51.8); "whoever robs the evil one of power or life" (46.4); "those who will lend me devo-

tion," etc. One can finally quote, after Schaeder,[23] two con-
trasting passages: "To you answered the Wise Lord, united
to Good Mind, through the Dominion, in sympathy with
sunlike Order: your beneficent, good Devotion do we choose
for ourselves; let her be ours" (32.2); "through the beneficent
Spirit and the best Mind, according to our actions and words
based on Order, may the Wise Lord bestow upon us Integrity
and Immortality with the Dominion of Devotion" (47.1). In
the first instance Order is on the divine side, Devotion on the
human; in the second instance they are reversed.

After Zoroaster this supple, delicate system was lost. The
Entities were reduced to mere deities, which were even separated into male and female. Nevermore was their name used
to designate a human faculty. They did nonetheless remain
charged with symbolism; but they had taken on new mean-
ings.

MITHRA

An explanation of Mithra-Mitra can be sought in the etymology of his name, which is clear ("the Contract"), and in the
hymns dedicated to him in the Veda (Rig. III.59) and the
Avesta (Yasht 10). This has recently been done by two scholars
working independently, Paul Thieme and Ilya Gershevitch.[24]
All the attributes and characteristics of the god can be reduced
to the idea of personified contract, from which they can all
be deduced by degrees. This is too easy a game, and one too
full of hazards: shall we say, for instance, that Mithra pro-

[23] *Gott und Mensch in der Verkündigung Zarathushtras* (1937); republ. *Der
Mensch in Orient und Okzident* (1960), pp. 94 ff.
[24] P. Thieme, *Mitra and Aryaman* (New Haven, Conn., 1958); I. Gershevitch,
The Avestan Hymn to Mithra (Cambridge, 1959).

cures "wide pastures" in order to reward respect of the contracts? Or to make it possible? And why should Contract have
white horses? By refusing all conparative construction and
"sticking to facts," one falls into arbitrary improvisations.

The facts are much better justified if one recognizes that
Contract is a new name given to an ancient god or, what
amounts to the same thing, a new god introduced into pre-
existing patterns, namely those of the tripartite ideology.
These alone allow us to take account of data such as those of
the Brahmanas, which oppose Mitra to Varuna like day to
night, like "this world" to "the other world," etc. These
oppositions, which have helped Dumézil, after Bergaigne and
Güntert, to reconstruct the two aspects of sovereignty, are rejected as irrelevant by Thieme and Gershevitch, who note
that they are attested only in more recent texts. But what do
the lacunae of the Rig Veda prove as against the concurring
evidence of many other Indo-European peoples?

Besides, the Mitra-Varuna opposition is already indicated,
showing the way the Brahmanas were to follow, in two passages of the Atharva Veda and at least one of the Rig Veda[25]—
so much so that the Rig Veda, in its relative silence, far from
representing the ancient state of things, the only legitimate
basis for a reconstruction, appears on the contrary to have
innovated in this.[26]

One can then give full value to the fact that Varuna is to
Mitra exactly as, in Iran, Asha is to Vohu Manah—Varuna

[25] Passages quoted by Kuiper in his review of Thieme's book in *Indo-
Iranian Journal* (1959), pp. 210 ff.
[26] Cf. Kuiper: "When the authors of the Brahmanas contrast Mitra (day)
with Varuna (night), we must assume that they had good reasons for doing
so, and that the real problem is rather, why the Rig Veda is silent about it."

and Asha more distant, Mithra and Vohu Manah nearer to man—as well as to the fact that, as Vohu Manah patronizes the ox, so is Mithra the god "with wide pastures."

The pair formed by Mitra and Varuna survives in Iran in the Avestan phrase *mithra ahura berezanta* ("the two great ones, Mithra and Ahura"). It is scarcely open to doubt that Ahura in this phrase was a designation of Varuna, who in India was the *asura* par excellence. His name is commonly specified in Iran by the epithet *mazda* ("wise"), rather similar to the adjective *medhira* which Rig Veda I.25.20 couples with Varuna. This does not mean that Ahura should have been wholly similar to Varuna, an opinion which has justly scandalized such scholars as Lommel and Gershevitch. The god was strongly differentiated as a result of the Iranian reform, but the divergence of the outcome does not preclude our tracing his origins back to a common starting-point.[27]

According to K. Barr,[28] Ahura Mazda is not a continuation of Varuna alone but of the whole pair Mitra-Varuna, the associate Mithra being replaced by the epithet mazda which characterized his near-to-man, providential action. However, if Ahura Mazda absorbed Mithra in this way (which would account for the latter's absence in the Gathas), one must note, at any rate, that the Achaemenids were no longer conscious of the fact, since they worshipped *Mesoromasdes*, i.e., Mithra and Ahuramazda.[29]

Barr would see in this merger of Varuna and Mitra into

---

[27] In this way we shall be able to dispense with the subtle hypotheses put forth by Gershevitch, *The Avestan Hymn*, pp. 47 ff.

[28] *Avesta* (in Danish; 1954), pp. 37, 208.

[29] Plutarch, *Ad principem*, explained by Wikander in *Orientalia Suecana* (1951).

one god the imprint of Zoroaster's genius and a proof that
Ahura Mazda was first proclaimed by this prophet. However, no positive fact allows us to decide whether or not Ahura
Mazda existed before Zarathushtra's reform. What seems more
certain is that Zarathushtra enriched and exalted him by
associating entities with him which had previously been independent.

AIRYAMAN

Mitra had two associates, Aryaman and Bhaga, the former of
whom survived in Iran, if not in the Gathas (which ignore
him as they ignore Mithra himself), at least in the Gathic
prayer *Airyema ishyo*. In contradistinction to Bhaga, who was
chiefly concerned with goods, Aryaman seems to have been
in charge of maintaining the society of *arya* people to whom
he owed his name. This is why the Zoroastrian prayer invokes
him "to help the men and women (disciples) of Zarathushtra."[30]

In Zarathushtra's system, Airyaman seems to have disappeared and made room for Sraosha, as Bhaga for Ashi.

ZURVAN

Zurvan is first attested in western Iran, outside Zoroaster's
horizon. The most ancient testimonies are admittedly somewhat ambiguous. The name Zurvan figures in Nuzi tablets
(thirteenth–twelfth centuries B.C.), but nothing tells us that he

[30] The interpretation given by Bailey, *Transact. Philological Society* (1959),
pp. 86 ff., "possessor, hence dispenser of riches (arya)," ignores the distinction
of meaning established by Dumézil between Aryaman and Bhaga.

was a "high god."[31] A Luristan plaque preserved in the Cincinnati Museum seems to represent a god of time with two twins.
To name the latter, as Ghirshman does,[32] Ohrmazd and Ari-
man is doubtless an anachronism, for it was only several centuries after the probable date of this bronze that Ohrmazd was
identified with the Beneficent Spirit, the adversary of the Destructive One. But these may well be the mythical twins.
whatever their name, whom Zoroaster presupposed as well
known and in whom he saw the two primeval Spirits.

The first text explicit enough and relatively well dated is
the excerpt from Eudemus of Rhodes preserved by Damascius,
the Neo-Platonist. Damascius raises the question, what the
ancient Iranians understood as the Intelligence and the Infinite All. And he answers, following Eudemus, that according to some of them it was Time, according to others Space,
from which Ohrmazd and Ahriman had been born, either
directly or after light and darkness.

Thus the importance of time in Iranian speculation is attested in the fourth century B.C. On the contrary, time holds a
very small place in the Avesta, despite the epithet designating
it as an autonomous god. This inconspicuous role may be
due to systematic avoidance. And Zoroaster's silence may also
be voluntary, for he likewise ignored Mithra.

In the latter Avesta, Zurvan is mentioned either as maker
of paths leading to the hereafter (Videvdat 19.29), a role
analogous to that of Vayu, the god of wind, elsewhere, or as
Infinite Time together with Thwasha and Vayu. Moreover, a
distinction is made in Yasna 72.10 between Zurvan *akarana*

---

[31] It can even be doubted, with Bailey, that the syllables considered really
designated a god.
[32] *Artibus Asiae* (1958), pp. 37 ff.

("Infinite Time" and Zurvan *darego-xvadata* ("Time with the long dominion"). This implies a certain theory of the production of time, which will be put forward in the Pahlavi works: Time of the long dominion proceeds from Infinite Time, lasts for twelve thousand years, and goes back to it.[33]

A passage in the Denkart commenting on the Gathic text about the two Spirits (Yasna 30.3) condemns the doctrine according to which Ohrmazd and Ahriman are brothers in the womb of the same mother. Earlier in the third century A.D., a Manichaean hymn condemned the same doctrine. But in Iran at the time when their prophet preached, it was Zurvan, not Ohrmazd, who occupied this position. The question of the relationship between Zurvanism and Mazdaism will be dealt with further on.

The Zurvanists delved further into the problem of evil, which was not sufficiently clarified, they thought, by Zoroaster's myth of the Choice. In Eznik's testimony, of the two twins who were born from Zurvan after he had sacrificed for a thousand years, Ohrmazd was the result of that sacrifice, Ahriman the result of a doubt which came to Zurvan concerning its efficacy.[34] Amongst Shahrastani's Zurvanians, some thought that Zurvan, born from light, doubted, and that from this doubt Satan was born; others professed the doctrine preserved by Eznik; yet others believed that there was constantly something bad in God—an evil thought or a corruption—and that this was the origin of Satan. As for the Gayomarthians of the same author, they professed that Ahriman was born from the idea which God had of the possibility of an Adversary.

---

[33] Zaehner, *Zurvan*, pp. 106 ff.
[34] See J. de Menasce, *Journal Asiatique* (1953), p. 307.

Zurvanistic speculation set great store on divine quadrinity. We know it through several Syriac testimonies which cite, along with Zurvan, three other names, Ashoqar, Frashoqar, and Zaroqar, given as other gods but really hypostases of the first one. As noted by Nyberg,[35] *ashoqar* and *frashoqar* are ancient Avestan epithets, *arso-kara* ("making virile") and *frasho-kara* ("making splendid"), and *zaroqar* is a plausible substitute for yet another Avestan adjective, *marsho-kara* ("making old"). The three names characterize time in its relationship to three moments of the human life: youth, maturity, old age.

That we have really to do with a tetrad is confirmed by the Manichaean tradition which designates Zurvan, the supreme god, "father of greatness," as a four-faced god (*tetraprosopos*).[36] But Zurvan's quadrinity manifested itself under yet other forms, which Zaehner has studied in detail. Thus the anonymous Syrian author brings the above-mentioned tetrad into relationship with the four elements. The most interesting tetrad is that associating light, power, and wisdom with Zurvan, for this seems to be the origin of the Mazdean tetrad.

Has Zurvan a counterpart in Indian religion? The Indian speculation on time (kala) represents recent developments and cannot be projected back into the Indo-Iranian past.[37] But India had another high god, Prajapati, whose history is remarkably parallel to Zurvan's. As Zurvan offered sacrifice in the beginning, in order to obtain an offspring, so Prajapati,

---

[35] "Questions de cosmologie et de cosmogonie mazdéennes," *Journal Asiatique* (1931), p. 221.

[36] Migne, *Patrologia graeca*, I.1461; Kessler, *Mani*, p. 403; cf. Zaehner, *Zurvan*, p. 54.

[37] Scheftelowitz, *Die Zeit als Schicksalsgottheit in der indischen und iranischen Religion* (1929).

the high god, was the first to perform the *daksayana* offering for the same purpose. It is therefore probable that as early as the Indo-Iranian period a myth told how, before creation, a high god offered sacrifice out of craving for progeny.[38] It is by no means certain that in this ancient form of the myth the god gave birth to twins, for of this there is no trace in India. But between the two traditions there is a minute concordance which to my knowledge has not been noted and which confirms the antiquity of the myth. Zurvan, while offering sacrifice, had a doubt. Similarly, Prajapati "practised burning austerities; . . . he wiped his forehead and it was ghee. He held it forth to the fire and was seized by a scruple: Should I offer it? Should I not?"[39]

The similarity of the myth concerning Zurvan and Prajapati gives emphasis to the fact that if Prajapati is not properly Time, the Lord of creatures, the primeval being, he is nevertheless identified not only with the Sacrifice and the Spirit but also with the Year.

MAZDAISM AND ZURVANISM

In the Sassanid period all the documents of Christian or Manichaean origin that inform us concerning Mazdaism attack the belief in Zurvan as the essential dogma of this religion. In this they contradict the native Mazdean testimon-

---

[38] This refutes, as shown by Widengren, *Religionens Värld* (2d. edn., 1952). p. 71, Schaeder's hypothesis put forward in *Zeitschr. d. deutsch. Morgenl. Gesellsch.* (1941), pp. 290 ff., that the myth of Zurvan as father of Ohrmazd and Ahriman was but a malignant invention of Christians.

[39] Taittiriya Brahmana 2.1.2.1–3, cited by Sylvain Lévi, *La doctrine du sacrifice dans les Brahmanas* (1899), p. 28.

ies, which almost completely ignore Zurvanism. How can we explain this contradiction, this "problem of Zurvanism"?

Richard Frye in a recent article[40] seems to have thrown considerable light on the question. According to him, Zurvanism and Mazdaism were in their beliefs two religions, but in their practices one. There is no proof of the existence of a Zurvanite cult or church. One can only imagine, inside the Mazdean church, especially at the royal court, Zurvanite groups.

This variation of doctrine is reflected, we will add, in the testimony of the Christians. This testimony is indeed not unanimous: it does not always designate Zurvan as the supreme god, but sometimes Ohrmazd under the name "Zeus," or "great Zeus,"[41] sometimes (and more often) Mihr, under the name "Sun,"[42] sometimes both.[43]

In that view of Frye's, the decline of Zurvanism after the Muslim conquest is accounted for by the decline of the Sassanid ruling class: the latter, the court, the *dihqans,* and certain *mobads* embraced Islam in order to retain a crumb of power by collaborating with the conquerors. It is probably they who introduced into Islam the time speculation which looms so large in it under the Abbassids.

However, this hypothesis does not exhaust the problem: we still have to clarify the relationship between Zurvan and Ohrmazd. It is not sufficient to say that Ohrmazd is the son

[40] "Zurvanism Again," *Harvard Theological Review* (1959), pp. 65 ff.
[41] Acts of Sabha and Mu'ain.
[42] Elisée, in Langlois, *Historiens de l'Arménie,* II, 197, 234; Acts of Simon Barsabba'e, Bedjan II, 131 ff.
[43] Under the names of Mihr and Bel, Theophylactos IV. 16.5.

of Zurvan, etc. According to Bianchi,[44] Zurvan is the initial god, Ohrmazd the sovereign god, as are Ouranos and Zeus respectively.

Father de Menasce sees this relationship differently. In a lecture delivered at the Musée Guimet in 1959 but as yet unpublished,[45] he defines Zurvan as a First One with nothing determined—a little like what there was at the origin according to Hymn 10.129 of the Rig Veda—but a First One who will give birth to what is determined. He is not a creator god, and that is his supreme and characteristic "quality"; he needs children in order to create. In that sense he is rather "undetermined" than "beyond good and evil." That is how it is explained that he should have become the great god of Manichaeism, for Manichaeism essentially loathes creation; but this is not at all the Mazdean attitude.

Symbolism as a Game

Pahlavi literature offers a unique example of symbolism as a sort of game. It is the small piece entitled *Daruk i Xorsandih* ("The Medicine of Contentment"), reproduced in Asana's *Pahlavi Texts*. Here is a summary of it, as given by the editor on page 50 of his Introduction:

It prescribes a recipe, measuring one dram, which is very beneficial to the body and the soul. The six drugs to be mixed in equal measure are as follows: one *dang* weight of "mixing contentment with meditation and recognizing it with wisdom"; one *dang* of "if I do not do this, what shall I do?"; one *dang* of "I ought to be

---

[44] *Zaman i Ohrmazd* (1958), p. 242.
[45] But a summary of it has appeared in *"A Locust's Lef," Studies Taqizadeh* (1962), pp. 182 ff.

good from this day till to-morrow" ("Take care of to-day, and to-morrow will take care of itself"); one *dang* of "Perhaps my condition will be worse than this"; one *dang* of "It is very comfortable for me to be content with what I have"; and one *dang* of "If I be not contented, it is not good for action and very discomfortable to me." These drugs are to be made in the mortar of patience, to be pounded with the pestle of devotion and to be strained through the silk cloth of "beturih" [faith]; two spoonfuls with the spoon of "Confidence in God" should be taken every day early in the morning; the water of "ought to be done" is to be taken just after it.

II
The Ritual

THE KUSTI

Every young Parsee has to be initiated, at an age varying between seven years (in India) and ten (in Iran), in a ceremony consisting essentially in investing him or her with the shirt (*sadre*) and the thread (*kusti*). This rite recalls the Brahmanic initiation. But the cord of the *Brahmans* is of relatively recent date: originally it was a flap of garment worn over the left shoulder and under the right armpit. It seems that parallel developments took place in India and Iran from a common basis.

"It is enjoined," says Modi (*Religious Ceremonies*, p. 177), "that, excepting the time of bathing, a Zoroastrian must always bear the sacred shirt and thread. The thread is to be untied and retied during the day on the following occasions: (1) Immediately after leaving bed in the morning; (2) Every time after answering a call of nature; (3) Before saying prayers; (4) At the time of bathing; (5) Before meals. . . . The Datastan i Denik says that, from times immemorial, men turn towards light at the time of performing the kusti ceremony as it is connected with a form of prayer."

A variegated symbolism is attached to the kusti: it was the subject of a small treatise, the Cim i kustik, and it is also dealt with in chapter 40 of the Datastan i Denik and in the Persian work Sar-name i raz i Yazdani.

It is a sign of obedience, since a servant, in order to execute commands, "girds up his loins" (as the Bible states); it is also a symbol of the division of the body into a noble part, above, and an ignoble one, underneath. Both interpretations are given in the Cim i kustik.

We have already seen that in the Avesta the girdle was figured in the sky by the Milky Way and that it "was" the good Mazdean religion. Two recent interpretations play on the etymology: the kusti is what shows the right direction (*kust*); or it is a boat (*kashti*) carrying us to the haven of bliss.[1]

In its very structure the kusti is also charged with symbolism: "The 72 threads composing the kusti symbolize the 72 *has* or chapters of the Yasna. The 24 threads which make up each of the three tassels at each end of the kusti symbolize the 24 *kardas* or sections of the Vispart, a part of the liturgical prayer; the six strands, each of twelve threads, into which the 72 threads of the kusti are divided at the time of weaving are said to symbolize the six religious duties of a Zoroastrian (celebration of season festivals, funeral ceremonies, prayers three times a day in honor of the sun, and three times a month in honor of the moon, etc.); the twelve threads in each of the six strands symbolize the twelve months of the year; the six tassels symbolize the six season festivals; the hollow of the thread symbolizes the space between this world and the

[1] Modi, *The Religious Ceremonies and Customs of the Parsees*, 2d. edn., (1937), pp. 173 ff.

next; the doubling of the thread in the beginning symbolizes the connection between the present corporeal world and the future spiritual world; the turning of the kusti inside out symbolizes the passage of the soul from the corporeal to the spiritual world; the final knitting of all the threads into one symbolizes universal brotherhood or union."

Since the girdle is given to every one as he enters life, it is natural that on the day of Resurrection Ohrmazd should (according to Bundahishn 34.29) hold the girdle in his hand, apparently in order to invest the blessed with it.

The knots one makes in the girdle when putting it on are also symbolic: "Knots, which signify firmness and resolution," writes Modi (p. 178), "symbolize here resolutions about certain moral and religious thoughts. While forming the first half of the first knot in front on the second round of the thread, a Zoroastrian has to think that Ahura Mazda exists, that he is one, holy and matchless. While forming the second half of this first knot, he has to remember that the Mazdayasnian religion is the word of God and that he must have full faith in it. In the third round of the thread, while forming the first half of the second knot at the back, one has to remember that Zoroaster is the prophet of God, and that he is our guide to show us the proper path of worship. While forming the second half of the second knot, he is to bear in mind that he has always to attend to good thoughts, good words and good deeds."

THE SADRE, OR SHIRT, AND OTHER GARMENTS

The shirt should be white, a symbol of innocence, but above all, as will be seen in the next chapter, a symbol of religion;

it must be made of simple fabric, not double, because, according to the Datastan i Denik, Vohu Manah "is a creation, the first one," a statement which is far from clear.

The soul dons after death a white, luminous garment which, like the sadre worn by the living, is, as we have seen, the garment of Vohu Manah. The latter is described by Zatspram:[2] "Then he saw Vohu Manah, the Amesha Spenta, in the shape of a man, handsome and brilliant. . . . He had put on and wore a garment which was like silk, on which there was no section and no seam, because its substance was light, and his height was nine times as much as Zarathushtra." The shirt is made of two pieces, one in front, one behind, symbolizing the past and the future. About the fold made by the shirt on the breast, Modi writes: "The *gire-ban* is known as the *kisse i kirfe*, i.e., the purse of righteousness. It indicates symbolically that a man has to be industrious, and has not only to fill his purse or bag with money, but also with righteousness." According to the Shayast ne Shayast, the shirt must be worn directly on the skin. Thus, Modi concludes, "the sudre is a symbol that reminds one of purity of life and of righteousness."

An obvious symbolism is attached to new garments, signs of purity and renewal. The candidate to a great purification of *bareshnum,* a ceremony we shall describe further on, strips himself of his old garments and buries them. In the ceremonies at the end of the year new garments are retailed. The initiation of the priest includes putting on a new costume, which in this case is white, the color of religion; moreover, the candidate puts on a white turban and carries in his left hand a

---

[2] Zatspram 21.8; after Widengren, *Vohu Manah* (1945), p. 89.

shawl and in his right a *gurz* or club, representing Mithra's
weapon.

The garment of the soul is a frequent theme in Pahlavi
literature. In the Menok i Xrat, chapter 43, the virtues that
help combat evil are the garments, the weapons, and the
armor of the faithful: "To confound Ahriman the wicked and
the demons, and to escape from hell, the dark, the evil-
smelling, is possible if they make the spirit of wisdom a shield
for the back; and wear, on the body, the spirit of contentment like a coat of mail and valor; and the spirit of thankful-
ness, like a club; and the spirit of devotedness, like a bow;
and the spirit of liberality, like an arrow; and the spirit of
moderation, like a javelin; and the spirit of perseverance, as
a gauntlet; and the spirit of destiny they advance as a protection."

In the Denkart persons are mentioned who walk the paths
of righteousness. One reads of the "garment of their good
self," whereas those who were born under the evil Mars
"wear their stubborn self as appropriate garment" (Madan
203). In another passage: "The religion is the wisdom of his
self [Mazda's] and his garment is the goodness, his ornament
the truth and his worthy creatures the mazda-worshippers.
. . . Ahriman's religion is the foolishness of his self and his
garment is Vice."

In Manichaeism, primeval man, Ohrmizd, in his struggle
with the demons of darkness, puts on as an armor the five
elements—fire, water, light, wind, and space.

The metaphor of the garment is already current in the
Bible, both in the Old and the New Testament: "For he
[Yahweh] put on righteousness as a breastplate, and a helmet

of salvation upon his head; and he put on the garments of vengeance for clothing, and was clad with zeal as a cloak" (Isaiah 59.17). And in the Epistle to the Ephesians, 6.14–17: "Stand therefore, having your loins girt about the truth, and having on the breastplate of righteousness; and your feet shod with the preparation of the gospel of peace; above all, taking the shield of faith, wherewith ye shall be able to quench all the fiery darts of the wicked. And take the helmet of salvation and the sword of the Spirit, which is the word of God."

Before putting on glorified garments in the hereafter, in his world the soul is clad in a garment of flesh (Datastan i Denik, folio 138^{v}, line 5). After death, as she rises towards the sky of Ohrmazd, the soul is welcomed by Vohuman and receives a crown and a garment. The Artag Viraf Namak, which describes the torments of hell and the bliss of heaven, gives the pious souls garments embroidered in gold and silver; to their wives, garments so embroidered and enriched with precious stones; to the warriors, garments of gold covered with precious stones, well adorned and embroidered. In the hereafter, as earlier on earth when putting on the sadre, man has to identify himself with Vohu Manah, which means, he must clothe himself in light.[3]

An analogous conception, appearing in India, seems to warrant the ancient origin of the theme, as shown by Wikander.[4] The Apsarases who, as we have seen, come to meet the soul, carry among other things garlands and robes. They adorn the soul as Brahma himself, i.e., they clothe it in the

[3] Widengren, *The great Vohu Manah and the Apostle of God* (1945), p. 50.
[4] Vayu (1941), p. 47.

world-mantle. This would at the same time warrant the high antiquity in Iran (despite the silence of the Avesta) of the conception which appears in Manichaeism, in the Gnostics, and in Christianity.

In Manichaeism, the soul of the deceased puts on marvelous garments. Mani, according to a Turfan text, "seized a divine garment, the diadem of light and the beautiful crown."

It is a current conception with the Gnostics that the soul, coming down to earth, traversed the seven planetary circles successively, clothing herself in each with the various qualities of her terrestrial condition, of which she will strip herself again when going up again, after death, from sphere to sphere until she joins god.

In the Christian sources the comparison of the body of resurrection with a heavenly garment is found, for instance, in the Ethiopian Enoch, (62.15ff.), in Corinthians II (5.1ff.), and in four passages of Revelation (3.4ff., 6.11, 7.9, and 19.8): "They shall walk with me in white for they are worthy. He that overcometh, the same shall be clothed in white raiment"; "And white robes were given unto everyone of them"; "They stood before the throne, and before the Lamb, clothed with white robes, and palms in their hands"; "And to her was granted that she should be arrayed in fine linen, clean and white: for the fine linen is the righteousness of saints."

THE BARESHNUM OR GREAT PURIFICATION

The great ceremony of *bareshnum* is peculiar in that its symbolism partially escapes the ingenuity of the interpreters. Thus Khurshed Dabu writes: "No clues are given to explain the ground-plan." That is perhaps because this ceremony has remained close to magic.

The candidate to purification formerly placed himself successively on holes made in the ground and called *magas*; they are now replaced by groups of five flat stones. The holes were obviously destined to receive and pass on to the soil the impurities of which the candidate stripped himself by rubbing himself with *gomez,* sand, and water. These holes or groups of stones are surrounded at some distance with furrows traced in rectangles, whose pattern is puzzling to the interpreter. But the aim of the furrow itself is clear: it is to limit the zones of pollution in which the disinfection is carried on. As Modi writes (p. 109): "The furrows are supposed to be trenches which would prevent the polluted water from his infected body to run beyond that limit." And he adds: "The *karsha* (furrow) that a corpse-bearer draws round about the corpse in the house before removing the body to the Tower is of a similar kind." For the corpse is the impure object par excellence, and, indeed, it is essentially to purify oneself from touching a corpse that one undergoes the *bareshnum.*

What is sacred, like what is impure, is circled off, for the two notions are originally one. A space marked off as sacred is called *pavi,* a word meaning literally "washed." In the room where the fire is maintained and in the one where sacrifices are performed in the presence of fire, the places for the fire-vase and the officiating priests are surrounded with drains forming a rectangle or a square and serving to gather and evacuate the waters with which these sacred places are, periodically, ritually cleansed. These rectangular drains are perhaps the origin of the rectangles in the *bareshnum,* which would then repeat out of doors the interior disposition of a temple. But this explanation is not found in the Parsee commentators, who indeed know of none.

The priest hands the candidate water, sand, and *gomez* in a spoon fixed to the end of a nine-knotted stich. "Perhaps it was thought," Modi writes wistfully (p. 111), "that, in case the infection escaped from the infected person who is a candidate for purification, it might not reach the purifying priest (who always stays outside the furrows) and might be stopped at every knot of the stick. It might pass through the fibres of the stick but might be stopped at each of the knots." And he adds: "All this is symbolic, however we may try to understand it." But if this is symbolic, then what is not? It seems obvious, on the contrary, that this ceremony corresponds to a wholly physical conception of impurity.

This physical conception also dominates another custom, this time in so manifest a fashion that the Parsees do not even raise the question of its symbolic value. I am referring to the priests' custom of covering their mouths each time they say prayers before the fire or in front of offerings or other sacred objects, in order not to soil them with their spittle.

The *bareshnum* requires the presence of a dog, which is led up to the candidate several times to be touched by him with his left hand, on the left ear. This dog must be "four-eyed," viz. he must have two spots underneath the eyes, a peculiarity supposed to double the efficiency of his gaze. In the funeral rite also a four-eyed dog is led into the presence of the deceased person.

This practice, called *sagdid* ("dog sight"), is diversely interpreted, at least in its funereal function: the dog is supposed to feel or smell if the person is still alive; the eyes of the dog have a magnetic power; the dog is present on account of his loyalty, for the services he has rendered to the living person; dogs eat dirty food: their presence may symbolize the destruction of immoral passions (Modi, *Religious Ceremonies,* p. 129).

In Vedic religion, when the horse to be sacrificed is bathed, it is required that a low-caste man should kill with a club a "four-eyed" dog, which probably symbolizes the hostile powers. The difference between this rite and the *sagdid* is accounted for by the Mazdeans' veneration of the dog.

One can scarcely separate the funerary *sagdid* from the belief in the two dogs which, according to Videvdat 13.9, keep the Bridge of the Retributor and which in turn have their opposite numbers in India (Rig Veda 10.14.2; Atharva Veda 18.3.13) in the two "four-eyed" dogs, messengers of the death god Yama.[5]

The dog's gaze, in the *sagdid,* has an effect opposite to that of the evil eye. The latter is described in Videvdat 18, a propos of the *jahi,* the prostitute whose gaze "dessicates a third of the waters, stops in their growth a third of the plants, causes to disappear in the faithful a third of the good thoughts, good words, good deeds, etc."

The *gomez,* a term usually translated by "beef's urine," is really, as already prescribed in the Videvdat, bull's urine, supposedly partaking of the fecundating power of the sperm. It is a source of life that is employed to combat the impurity which death has caused.

The *bareshnum* can only be performed by day, not at

---

[5] Lommel, *Die Religion Zarathushtras,* p. 190; Wolfgang Voigt, *Die Wertung des Tieres in der zarathushtrischen Religion* (München, 1937), p. 50.

night, and only during the dry season; the rains could spread the impurity.

Generally speaking, the *bareshnum* puts the priest who undergoes it in a state of ritual purity which renders him apt to celebrate the ceremonies of the fire temple: Yasna, Visprat, Videvdat and Baj. But he may lose this state if he commits one of the following infractions: (1) eating food prepared by non-Parsees; (2) not observing the Baj or "grace"; (3) making long journeys by land or sea;[6] (4) swearing or taking an oath; (5) dropping his turban from his head. In all these cases he will have to undergo a new *bareshnum*.

In fact the priests often submit themselves to the *bareshnum* without necessity. The rite has become a sort of prelude to that of the Yasna, etc., and it is performed, like the latter, for the benefit of the person who pays the priest or for whom he is paid. From "purificatory," the ceremony has thus become more vaguely beneficent.

One must stress the fact that the distinction between purification rites and rites to promote well-being, fecundity, etc., is not as sharply drawn as one might think. *Gomez,* the purifying agent par excellence, is also a vital fluid. If it efficiently combats impurity, notably that which results from the contact of a dead body, that is because it is a life essence.

FLOWERS, PERFUMES, HANDSHAKE

The rite of flowers, performed by two priests facing each other, holds an important place in the ceremony of *Afringan,* or "benedictions," intended to invoke the blessings of the En-

---

[6] This custom was abolished in 1922; cf. Modi, preface to the *Darab Hormazyar Framarz's Rivayat* ed. M. R. Unvala (Bombay, 1922).

tities and address vows to the deceased and the authorities. It requires eight flowers, which the priests arrange in two columns on a tray between themselves, leaving the fire between the tray and the *raspi,* the priest who ranks as inferior. As they recite prayers, they hold the flowers in their hands or exchange them in a predetermined order, in gestures all supposed to be charged with symbolic value. According to Modi (p. 376), the recitation, flowers in hand,

seems to indicate that, as there is one God above to rule over the world, there must be one king here as his representative to rule over the country. He must be powerful enough to overrule all impiety, injustice, misrule, oppression and immorality.

As for the exchange of flowers, it symbolizes the exchange of lives between this world and the next. Souls are born and souls pass away. How do they do so? That is indicated and symbolized by the next process in connection with the flowers. The priests recite twice the prayer *Humatanam,* etc. (Yasna 35), wherein are praised those who practice good thoughts, good words and good deeds.

Now the Parsee books say that a pious, righteous soul passes away to Paradise in four steps, first reaching the place of good thoughts—(the sphere of the stars), secondly the good words (the moon), thirdly the good deeds (the sun), finally Paradise in Eternal Light.

So, at this juncture, the *Zoti* (or principal priest), while reciting the above words *Humatanam,* etc., lifts up the three flowers on the right hand side, one by one, beginning from above; then, similarly on the other side, beginning from below. This process symbolizes the view that a pious soul has to come down to and moves about in this world and then to pass away from this world to the other: the triad of good thoughts, good words and good deeds. Having thus lifted up the two sets of three flowers with the above prayer praising goodness of thoughts, words and deeds, he gives them into the hands of the *raspi,* who in the end returns them to him.

He finally places them on one side in the tray. At the first recital of the *Humatanam* prayer and at the first lifting up of the flowers, the raspi stands on one side of the fire-vase, i.e. on the right hand side of the zoti, and, at the second recital, on the other side. He, thus, changes his situation, to symbolize the change of situation on the part of the soul, after death.

A very different meaning is read into this ceremony by Khurshed Dabu in his *Message of Zarathustra* (1956), pp. 139ff. He sees in it "a silent dramatic course of instruction."

In esoteric philosophy, left-hand path is that of untruth; right-hand one is the correct righteous path. So there is polarity with two opposite paths to choose from. Imagine the two erect flowers (at the end of the two lines, near the *Zoti*) as suggesting the roots of good and evil. The three flowers on the *raspi's* left indicate good thoughts, words and deeds.

The raspi gets up as a disciple seeking instruction from the teacher. The latter offers him "the root of evil"—implying that the disciple should first eliminate evil source from his heart and mind, before "good seeds can be sown." After some prayers he comes to the teacher to his own left side—suggesting that he has mastered the root of evil (ignorance and illusion). The *Zoti* exchanges flower n. 2 (which he had held so long) with the *raspi's* offer of n. 1. It would mean that the disciple should now concentrate on the root of virtue (wisdom). The teacher offers him 3-4-5. The disciple, while receiving these, touches fire-censer with a shovel; and with a gesture suggests that he would burn these branches of evil. The disciple then goes over to his right (the *Zoti's* left), and there he is given 6-7-8. He bows to the fire and with 7 flowers in his hand (the store of experience) he contacts the teacher, who takes the end of his shovel and gives nine knocks on a water-pitcher at nine points. As the water symbolizes feelings, the knocks may signify all impacts and the directions of the heart's field. Then the disciple hands over all the 7 flowers in his hand (surrendering to the teacher all the fruits of experience) and then follows a peculiar grip with both hands exchanged between the two priests, etc.

We shall deal presently with the clasping of hands.

The different species of flowers, numbering thirty, were, according to Bundahishn 16, respectively associated with the thirty *yazatas* or deities presiding over the thirty days of the month; the myrtle-jasmine belonged to Ohrmazd, the white *saman* or clover to Vohuman, the basil to Shahrevar, the musk to Spandarmat, the lily to Xordat, etc. (A complete table is to be found in Modi, pp. 374ff.)

The ceremony of the perfumes, *dhup-sarvi,* has also a mystical sense. Modi writes (p. 415):

Fragrant flowers, rose-water and other perfumes are placed in trays on carpets on which the assembly is seated. At the end of the ceremony in honor of the dead, these flowers are distributed and the rose-water sprinkled among the persons assembled. Again, during the performance of the ceremony, fragrant wood like sandalwood and the agar, and fragrant incense like frankincense are burned.

Now, what do these perfumes of the fragrant flowers, rose-water and other odoriferous liquids seem to signify and symbolize? The ceremony seems to signify that the path of the righteous souls in the next world is besprinkled with fragrance and joy. It moralizes and says, as it were, to the people assembled: "A righteous soul that passes away to the next world has his way beset with fragrance and joy."

The ritual handclasp is performed in a peculiar way, with the palms held vertically and parallel to each other and each person holding in his own hands successively the other person's left, then right hand, then touching his own forehead with his fingertips.

Modi writes (p. 382):

From the fact that a *hamazor* (handclasp) was performed in the liturgical services with a view to signify participation and unity and with a wish that the person with whom it was performed may be righteous, the *hamazor* has come to signify a religious or solemn way of communicating one another's good wishes on the New Year's day. Early in the morning of that day, after washing and putting on new apparel, the male members of the family exchange this form of salutation. Friends do the same when they meet one another. . . .

. . . Behind the outward passing of hands in the *hamazor* which signify unity, harmony, participation, there lies the inner idea, which demands that the participants must unite in the works of righteousness. . . . There is not only the physical *hamazor* between man and man, but also a kind of spiritual *hamazor* between man and nature, between man and nature's God.

The simple handshake is represented on a relief of the Nimrud Dagh in Asia Minor, where it seems a symbol of the royal investiture given by the god Mithra to King Antiochus of Commagene. The father of this king, Mithridates, was figured at a small distance, in Arsameia on the Nymphaios, shaking hands with Heracles.

In the Mysteries of Mithras, shaking hands was part of the ritual: the initiation ended in a handshake with the *Pater*. In the sacred legend, on the Pettau (Yugoslavia) relief, Mithras and Sol are seen shaking hands over an altar, and on the relief of Virunum (Austria) Mithras shakes hands with Sol as he touches him on the shoulder with his left hand.

In the Manichaean myth, the Living Spirit, come to earth in order to rescue Primeval Man, holds out his hand to him and their handshake will become in the Manichaean Church a symbolic gesture.[7]

----

[7] Puech, *Le Manichéisme* (1949), p. 78 and n. 317.

FIRE

A fire is present at most rites: in the death-room, near the Tower of Silence, in the Yasna ceremony, etc. Its primitive role—according to a custom wide-spread among semisavage peoples (Oldenberg, *Religion du Veda,* p. 287)—seems to be to ward off evil spirits. A trace survives of another function— also very widespread—that of receiving the flesh or fat of the victims. On the third day after the funeral, a little animal fat is poured on the fire. The Nirangistan expressly states that the offerings of flesh and fat are made to the fire.

In the Yasna, the fire receives no solid or liquid offering, so that it might be thought to serve only as a witness, or as a perfumed source.[8] But such a view would involve forgetting that during the whole ceremony the priest faces the fire and that at several moments he explicitly addresses it (Yasna 35), looks at it, presents it with the *haoma,* etc. (Yasna 62).

Called the Fire of Ohrmazd, or the Son of Ohrmazd, the ritual flame may be considered the visible sign of the god's presence, the symbol of his true Order (*Asha*). Moreover, the fire of the highest grade, *Varhran* or *Bahram* fire, has the power to attract all the gods. This is stated in two Pahlavi texts (Denkart M 522.21 and Pahlavi Rivayat, Dhabhar 57.10). The *Varhran* fire appears there as a communication door between heaven and earth: when the celestial gods (*menokan yazatan*) come down to earth (in the *gete*), they first go to the *Varhran* fire, then to other places. Thus the sacrifice in front of the fire is addressed to the *yazatan* or *yazdan*. Since

[8] Such is Lady Drower's conclusion in "The role of fire . . . ," *Journal of the Royal Anthropological Institute* (1944), p. 89.

it is also, and above all, addressed to Ohrmazd, an equivalence was bound to be felt between the two terms, and that is why, in my opinion, Yazdan has become a synonym of Ohrmazd.

This *Bahram* fire, kept in the principal temples, is treated as a king: a crown is hung over it. Several Pahlavi texts (Kar Namak) call it the king of fires. Its installation is called enthronement. And this perhaps provides the explanation of a frequent design on the reverse of Sassanid coins. The fire altar is represented there with a lion's legs whose presence has never been interpreted. But they clearly seem calculated to give the altar the appearance of a throne (similar to that of Darius, for instance, on the reliefs at Persepolis and elsewhere), and, consequently, to give the fire the dignity of a king. (Fig. 3.)

We should perhaps interpret in the same fashion the throne-shaped lamps of the Muslim period, such as the one in the Detroit Museum:[9] they could attest the survival into Islam of the Iranian veneration of the royal fire. When the *Bahram* fire is fed—five times a day—the logs are built into the shape of a throne.[10]

That the sacred fire should constantly be kept burning, that it is considered criminal to let it die, is not a peculiar trait of the Iranian religion. The same rule prevails, for instance, in the cult of Vesta, and it seems probable that the cult of the domestic fire had already developed in this way in the Indo-European period. The care with which the Mazdeans tend the fire is, at least in part, older than the

[9] Figs. 4 and 4a: original pictures communicated by the Detroit Museum. By courtesy of the Museum.

[10] Picture in Dabu, *The Message of Zarathustra*, p. 97, reproduced here, Fig. 5.

Iranian nation. Thus, when they "purify" it, they designate this action by a word of Indo-European origin: *yaozhda*.[11]

Nevertheless, fire-tending has certainly undergone a particular extension in Iran. We may ask to what end? In his book on the fire-priests,[12] Wikander drew a fundamental distinction between, on the one hand, the common rite in which the fire is used to burn the victims and receive the libations, and on the other hand the rite of keeping the fire for its own sake and giving it its own cult. Wikander holds that this second rite is new and is attached, not to the cult of Mazda, but to that of Anahita. But he has not succeeded in proving a special connection betwen Anahita and this particular ritual.

Concerning the care of the sacred fire, we are informed by Pahlavi and Persian texts and by the current usage. The texts describing the fire ritual—studied notably by the good Parsee scholar Tavadia (*Archiv für Religionswissenschaft* [1939], pp. 256ff.)—appear to be obscure and contradictory. According to Kamdin Shapur's Rivayat, the flame alone is carried along to a superior fire, and from thence to the fire of the highest rank of *Bahram* fire. This transfer of the flame is analogous to the repeated operations leading to the foundation of a new fire.

On the contrary, according to the Pahlavi Rivayat, "When fire is used and the work is done, fire must be collected. One must take a flame and place it elsewhere and carry the remnant (*aparik*) along to the embers of the *Varhran* fire."

---

[11] Dumézil, "A propos de latin jus," *Revue d'Histoire des Religions*, 134 (1947–48), 95 ff.
[12] S. Wikander, *Feuerpriester in Kleinasien und Iran* (1946).

It will be seen that according to this older text it is not the flame but, on the contrary, the remainder, the glowing embers which are transported.

How are we to explain this discrepancy? Tavadia is embarrassed, so much so that he hesitates in proposing his translation of the Persian Rivayat. I wonder if, in reality, this text did not combine two traditions which we might unravel in this way: a first rite is a purification of fire by refinement, with transfer of the flame only and its reunion with others similar to it, with a view to founding a superior fire. This is the rite developed by the Parsees.

The other is a regeneration of fire through transfer of the worn-out fire (viz. of its glowing embers, without the flame) to a superior fire already existing. The inferior fire is brought back to its master, so to speak, in order to renew its virtue. This recalls the custom, current all over the world, of the renewal of fires on New Year's eve; and indeed it seems probable that, to give the rite its full meaning, it had to be completed by returning the fire once again to the hearth from which it had been taken.

Be that as it may, this rite was dropped by the Parsees; but it seems to have been important under the Sassanids. We can see how vital its role must have been: to maintain in act, through a frequently repeated symbolic operation, the dependence of the hearths upon the village centers, of these upon the provinces, in brief, the whole political pyramid. It is not a mere chance that the highest fire should generally have been called the *Bahram* fire, i.e., the king of fires, in both the Pahlavi and Persian Rivayats.

We can understand why, when the Parsees went into exile, they abandoned this rite together with the political organization it symbolized. Later, when contact had been re-established with Iran in the eighteenth century, the Qadimis wanted to revive this practice. By then, this rite of regeneration had long since merged with that of purification by refining.

What then do the Parsees do, one may ask, when they have finished using a fire, if they do not transfer its embers and if it is forbidden to put it out? They follow the alternative usage prescribed by the Pahlavi Rivayat: they cover up the fire in order to let it smoulder on under the ashes until the next morning.

The ceremonies of the foundation of a fire have remained long and elaborate. The *Bahram* fire is the result of the collection, purification, and consecration of other, profane fires, numbering seventeen, which have been put to a variety of uses and thereby more or less soiled.

Since the final aim of all these manipulations is to obtain as pure a fire as possible, one wonders why they should include the most impure kind of fire conceivable, namely one with which a corpse has been burnt. The reason is probably because the rationale of the ceremony is also to deliver fire from its pollution, to save it. This would recall the process of delivering the light in the Manichaean religion.

Apart from the distinction between the *Bahram* fire, second-rank fires or *Adaran,* sufficient for a village with a dozen families, and the third-rank or domestic fires, *Dadgah,* there existed under the Sassanids a distribution of fires according to social classes.

A speculation connects the *Farnbag, Gushnasp,* and *Burzen-Mihr* fires respectively with the three social classes supposed to have been instituted by the three sons of Zoroaster; priests, warriors, and husbandmen. On the other hand the *Farnbag* fire seems to have been a Persian fire, whereas the *Gushnasp* fire was the ancient fire of the Median Magi. It is unfortunately not known for certain where the *Farnbag* fire was situated. The two versions of the Bundahishn disagree on this: the Indian one speaks of Kabul, the Iranian is corrupt. The latter, however, in the plausible interpretation given by Jackson,[13] locates this fire at Kariyan in Persia, on a naphta source. This is the fire Artaxsher visited before combating Artaban.

The *Gushnasp* fire was probably situated at Shiz (Taxt-i-Soleiman) in Azerbaijan. Of all the fires of the realm it held the highest rank, and it is likely that it had replaced the *Farnbag* fire in this exalted position when Artaxsher had vanquished Artaban and conquered the empire. In fact, Artaxsher sent presents to it. Varhran V, Khosrau I and Khosrau II deposited there the booty of their victories. There also, according to the Denkart, Shapur I had a copy of the Avesta deposited. Even if this is not exact, it implies an established fame as the religious center of the empire. "In sum," Christensen justly writes,[14] "this fire was the symbol of the monarchic and religious unity of the Sassanid kingship, strengthened by its alliance with the clergy." According to the Letter of Tosar, the Sassanids had reserved for themselves the right to keep at Ganjan (Ganzak, Shiz) the fire, a symbol of the supreme power.

The *Burzen-Mihr* fire never had the high rank of the other two. Unlike the king and the clergy, the peasants were never

[13] "The Location of the Farnbag fire," *Journal of the American Oriental Society* (1921), pp. 81 ff.
[14] *L'Iran sous les Sassanides*, 2d. edn., (1944), p. 167.

holders of sovereignty. Their fire was on Mount Revand, to the northwest of Nishapur.

Myths and legends are attached to the *Farnbag, Gushnasp* and *Burzen-Mihr* fires. The phenomenon called in the West "St. Elmo's fire" seems the basis of the legend that told how under the reign of Tahmuras, when the people emigrated "on the back of the Sarsok cow" to other parts of the world, and a tempest swept into the water the hearths placed on the back of that cow, the three fires shone instead and gave light to the people all through their crossing of the sea (Bundahishn 18). On Yima's murder, the *Farnbag* fire saved the "Royal Fortune" from the serpent Dahak. According to the Karnamak, Artaxsher, poisoned by his wife, was saved by the *Farnbag* fire which had taken the shape of a red rooster. When Kay Khosrau destroyed all the old idols, the *Gushnasp* fire descended onto the neck of his horse (an allusion to the name *Gushnasp, asp* meaning horse). Finally, the *Burzen-Mihr* fire performed miracles under the reign of Vishtasp, when Zoroaster proclaimed the new religion.

These traditions, as noted by Pagliaro in his "Notes on the History of the sacred fires of Zoroastrianism,[15] are obscure. This scholar has put forward a hypothesis as to their origin, trying to connect all three of them with Mithra. Now this is obvious as far as the third one is concerned, whose name clearly means "the great Mithra"; but it is more than doubtful for the others. One should in any case take account of the name of the fire-temples: *dar-i-Mihr* 'house of Mithra.' But this name can mean two things—either that the fire is really assimilated to Mithra, or that this building is not

[15] *Oriental Studies. . . . Pavry*, p. 378.

only used for the cult but also (as is the case) to dispense justice: for Mithra has not entirely lost his old value of god of contract; he is indeed still one of the three judges in the hereafter.

The three fires are not named in the Avesta, but they are alluded to in the section of it called Siroza.

The classifications studied so far, into three fires (*Farnbag, Gushnasp, Burzen-Mihr*) or into two (*Bahram, Adaran*), concern the ritual fires only. There is another, more general one, in which a physical speculation is reflected and which is at least as old as the other two, for it is already attested in the Avesta. It distinguishes between five fires: 1. *Berezisavah,* shining before the Lord; 2. *Vohufryana,* which burns in the body of men and animals; 3. *Urvazishta,* in the plants; 4. *Vazishta,* struggling with Spenjagrya in the clouds; 5. *Spenishta,* employed for work. This classification presupposes a physical doctrine on the universal presence of fire. But for the moment we must pass over the first and the last; we may observe that the other three (reading from the bottom up) form a system for the fire of lightning (that which fights with Spenjagrya, demon of the storm, among the clouds) brings on the rain that nourishes plants, from which we can get this fire by rubbing two pieces of wood,[16] and the plants nourish the animals and men in whom fire becomes vital heat. It would seem that a confusion arose between the first and the fifth fire, since *spenishta* (the name of the fifth fire) means, despite the definition given it, "the most sacred," which, rather, corresponds to the definition of the first fire.

These are very ancient speculations, even if they were

16 We read in the Pahlavi Rivayat that one of the difficult things God had to perform at creation was "to put fire into the plants without burning them up."

modified in the course of the centuries. For it is certainly no
mere chance if India, notably in the Chandogya-Upanishad,
also knows three sacrificial fires (*garhapatya*, "domestic fire";
anvaharya-daksina, "fire averting the demons"; *ahavaniya*,
"fire of the oblation of the gods") and five natural ones (*asau
loka*, the heavenly world, from which Soma is born; *parjanya*,
the storm, whence rain; *prthivi*, the earth, from which nourishment; *purusa, man,* from which sperm; *yosa,* woman,
whence the embryo)—speculations quite analogous to those
surviving in Iran.[17]

Legends on the origin of the fire cult were current in the
Middle Ages in the Christian Orient.[18] According to one,
reported among others by the Syriac Book of the Treasure
Cave and by the Book of Adam and Eve, Nimrud saw a fire
arise from the earth and he instituted its cult. Other legends
connect the fire with the gift made by Jesus to the Magi in
exchange for the presents they had brought to Bethlehem.
According to a Uigur text found at Bulayiq near Turfan,
Jesus gives them a stone. They weary of carrying it along and
end by throwing it into a pit and traveling on. But they see
a great glow in the sky and turn around: a flame is rising
from the pit. They understand then that the stone was divine
and that this fire is a fitting object of worship. In Mas'udi's
Golden Meadows it is Mary who rewarded the Magi for their
gifts by giving them a round bread. The Magi put it under
a stone; it disappears into the depths of the earth. A pit is
dug and two jets of fire spring up from it. These legends had

[17] Tavadia, "Middle Persian evidence for the Avestan conception of Fire,"
Studien . . . Wilhelm Geiger, p. 237, vainly attempted to verify the theory
brought forward by Hertel in a series of books, *Die Arische Feuerlehre*, etc.
[18] Ugo Monneret de Villard, *Le leggende orientali sui Magi evangelici*
(Rome, 1952).

spread in Syriac, Ethiopian, Arabic, and other versions, and Marco Polo came to know of them.

Fire was also an instrument of ordeal. The ordeal or judgment of God is no longer practiced by the Mazdeans. But it is abundantly attested in the Pahlavi books as well as in at least two passages of the Avesta. In section 3 of Yt. 12, Ahura Mazda orders the preparation of a *varah* (Avestan term for "ordeal"), in which fire, the *baresman*, butter, and the juice of plants are used. Chapter 4 of the Videvdat mentions two others kinds of ordeal, one (46) with boiling water, the other (54) with sulphur and gold water. The Gathas contain one reference to ordeal as an actual practice, besides several to a future ordeal at the end of time. According to Zatspram, the prophet subjected himself to the fire-ordeal in order to prove the excellence of his religion. That is no doubt a projection backward into the legendary past of a use for which we have at least one historical testimony: in the reign of Shapur II, Aturpat son of Mahraspand, to prove the truth of his doctrine, caused molten metal to be poured on his breast. The fact is reported in the Denkart and other Pahlavi texts.

According to the Denkart also (VII.V.4), there were thirty-three forms of ordeal; the Shayast ne Shayast distinguishes six "hot" ordeals (by fire, molten metal, boiling water, etc.) and cold ordeals (by poison, etc).[19]

The ordeal is a practice akin both to the oath and to divination. The phrase "to drink sulphur water" has remained in Persian a synonym of "to swear an oath." It is worthwhile mentioning that the Avesta contains a particular form of oath

[19] On Ordeal in general, see *Encyclopaedia of Religion and Ethics,* IX, 507 ff.; on ordeal in Iran, the article by Edwards, ibid., pp. 524 ff.

and also one of divination. In Yt 5.76–78, a divine favor is obtained by stating a truth: "if it is true that . . . , grant me. . . ." This is the equivalent of the Indian *satyakriya*. In Yt 14.43–45, when two armies are confronted, four feathers are thrown up between them. We are to understand that their position when falling will determine which camp is to be the winner.

The sun's rays must not fall on the fire, whose power would thereby be diminished (Dhabhar, p. 56). For the same reason, fire may not be brought to a fire, only "cooled fire" may. The faithful would content themselves with filing round the fire, in the corridor surrounding the room where it was burning. But there also seem to have been ceremonies where the fire was displayed, if one may judge by the tetrapyles, open on all four sides and placed on the summit of hills, as if to be seen from all points round about by night—and from as far as possible. No text mentions such a rite, but there seems no other way of justifying the choice of high places. Moreover, if the fire had been displayed by daylight, it is difficult to imagine that it was not touched by sunrays.

The visitors, after gazing at the fire and walking around it, receive a pinch of ashes that they apply to their forehead. According to Dabu (pp. 99ff.), "These ashes have several lessons to teach: (1) Humility—reminding one of the handful of dust that the physical body would yield ultimately; (2) Equality: all contributors, rich and poor, receive the same 'return.' Similarly the offerings of all visitors are received and consigned to the fire, without distinction. The resulting ashes reflect the lesson of all men being on the level; (3) Loyalty: the invisible "King" on the altar is worshipped as God's representative (called the Son), and it is an oriental custom to apply on the forehead (as sign of fidelity) dust from under the feet of a ruler; (4) Law of retribution: We offer our activities to the Recorder, and these are turned into corresponding rewards and re-actions. As you give, so do you receive: the fragrant wood is consumed, and the resultant is the pure ashes; (5) Magnetic vivifier: the ashes from the sacred altar are radiant with magnetic emanation. These, when applied to our vital centres (or plexuses) stimulate the life within, and purify our aura; (6) It is the token or voucher of acceptance of an offering, the only link between the Invisible Presence and the devotees who cannot enter the sanctum."

SACRIFICE (YASNA).

There survives only a feeble trace of blood sacrifice in the Parsee ritual. On the fourth day after the funeral, animal fat is cast into the sacred fire; the same rite is repeated at each season during the ceremonies of consecration of a *Bahram* fire. With the Zoroastrians of Persia, the Mihragan festival is celebrated with the sacrifice, in each house, of a goat or a sheep or a chicken.

The ancient books attest the earlier importance of blood sacrifice. It is especially relevant to the history of symbolism that the parts of the victim assigned to the god Haoma (the sacred liquor personified) corresponded to him in a symbolic fashion. He had reserved for him the jawbone and the left eye. Now, the left eye is the moon (as the right eye corresponds to the sun), and Haoma himself was, like Soma in India, currently identified with the moon.

Sacrifice, as it is practiced to-day, is essentially an offering

1. Darius I Tomb at Naqshi Rustam, near Persepolis (E. Schmidt, *Persepolis,* III, pl. 19)
Through the courtesy of Erich Schmidt and the University of Chicago Press

2 & 2a. Achaemenid seal (E. Schmidt, *Persepolis*, II, pl. 6)
Through the courtesy of Erich Schmidt and the University of Chicago Press

3. Kušana Gold Coin: Mozdooano, "Mazda Victorious"
Through the courtesy of Numismatic Society of America, New York

3a. Sasanian Coin: fire-altar in throne shape

4 & 4a. Lamp, Persian, XII century
Through the courtesy of Detroit Institute of Art

5. Fire-wood arranged as "throne" of the fire
Through the courtesy of New Book C⁰, Bombay

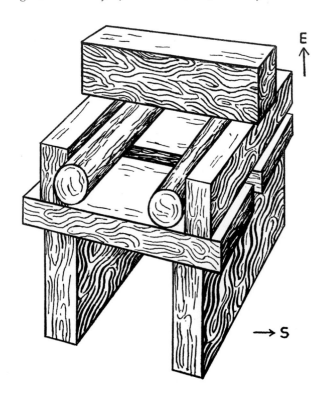

of haoma (the sacred liquor) before the sacred fire. "This ceremony, Manushcihr writes in his Datastan i Denik, Question 47, section 35, is so fraught with symbols of spiritual mysteries, of actions full of glory and splendor, that it would take too long to enumerate them."

Before offering and drinking the haoma, the latter has to be prepared. This occurs in a ceremony called *paragra*, comprising several auxiliary rites also taken over in the sacrifice proper:

(1) the *barsom* rite: the bundle of twigs is today replaced by metal twigs, but their name still recalls that of the *barhis*, the strewing of grass which served as a tablecloth in the Vedic sacrifice. In the course of the Parsee rite, sacred water is poured on the *barsom*. The symbolism of this operation is, according to Darmesteter (*Zend-Avesta*, I, 397) and approved by Modi (*Religious Ceremonies*, p. 266), perfectly clear: "The *barsom* represents vegetable nature, the sacred water represents the waters: it is put in contact with it in order to impregnate the whole flora with the virtues of water and to fecundate the earth." In the course of the ceremony, the sticks are put down several times on metallic stands terminating in lunar crescents, which confirms the magical, fecundating character of the rite. For the moon crescents are obvious symbols of vegetal fertility.

(2) the rite of the *aiwyaongham* or tie. It consists in washing a palm leaf in water ritually purified and dividing it into six fine strips, plaiting them together and tying the two extremities into knots: they are used in tying the *barsom*.

(3) the rite of the *urvaram* or "plant." A twig of pomegranate is washed in ritual water.

(4) the rite of the *jivam* or "living milk." A goat (a sub-

stitute for a cow) is milked. The consecration of milk is richly symbolic: Datastan, Question 47, 33–34.

(5) the rite of the *goshhudo*. This is the liturgical name of clarified butter, or ghee. It is used in manufacturing the *darun* and in buttering it.

(6) the rite of manufacturing the *darun,* the sacred bread. This will be eaten by the main priest, *zot*, at a certain stage of the sacrifice, and also by the other celebrants if they so wish.

The preparation of the haoma is itself a whole ceremony. Twigs of the haoma plant, *ephedra* (after which ephedrin is named), imported from Iran, are washed in the sacred water. They are then pounded in a mortar, the sides of which have previously been struck repeatedly by the pestle whilst apotropaic formulas were uttered. The demons are especially sensitive to the strokes on the northern side. The twigs are pounded together with the *urvaram,* or branch of pomegranate, with sacred water added; meanwhile, the priest recites the chief prayers of Parsism several times over. The juice is collected and filtered through a sieve made up of hairs of the sacred bull,[20] the whole action being accompanied by recitations, some of them in a suppressed tone. The juice so prepared is the *parahom,* or preliminary haoma, which will be consecrated in the course of the Yasna proper. The quadruple pressing of the haoma is interpreted by Manushcihr (Datastan 48.30) as an allusion to the four prophets, Zarathushtra and the three coming Saviors: Hoshetar, Hoshetarmah and the Saoshyant.

"The Yasna proper," writes Modi (p. 302), mostly consists

---

[20] This filtering is merely symbolical: the haoma is poured through a metal ring round which three, five, or seven hairs are twisted.

in the recital of the 72 chapters of the Yasna with some ritual here and there." Most of the time, the text has but a remote relationship with the rite it accompanies. Save a few exceptions, the correspondence is only between the main divisions. The ceremony requires two priests, the first of whom, the *zot,* is the sole reciter; the second, the *raspi,* from time to time pronounces the responses, but his main function is to feed the fire during the ceremony.

Before beginning the first chapter, the two priests wash their hands and take their stand, barefooted. They then recite in suppressed tones the *dibache,* i.e., the enumeration of the deities associated with the ceremony and the designation of the person for whose sake it is going to take place. Three times, the *barsom* is removed from its crescent-shaped stands, sprinkled with sacred water, and put back again. This is repeated several times in the course of the recital of the first chapter.

Twelve phases can be distinguished in the ceremony, between which the chapters are distributed as follows:[21]

(1) Chapter one is made up of invocations to the various deities; chapter two "harnesses" the sacred water and the *barsom* and repeats, with variants, the enumeration in chapter one.

(2) Presentation of the *darun* (or *myazda,* "solid offering") and the *goshhudo.* Here begins the offering of bread. This section can form a distinct ceremony, funereal in character: the offering is then made to the archangel, Srosh, conductor of dead souls. Chapters three to seven enumerate these offerings

---

[21] After Modi, pp. 303 ff., Darmesteter, *Le Zend-Avesta,* I, 5 ff., and Drower, "The role of Fire in Parsi ritual," *Journal of the Royal Anthropological Institute,* (1944), pp. 75 ff.

and the deities to whom they are addressed. During chapter eight, the *darun* is partaken of.

(3) Chapters nine to eleven form the *Hom Yasht*, a eulogy of the haoma, and end with the drinking of the haoma which has been prepared in the preliminary ceremony (*paragra*). The *raspi* washes his hands, continues feeding the fire and, as he performs a movement of translation from east to west comparable to the sun's, he takes up the haoma cup, touches the *barsom* with it, and hands it to the *zot*, who drinks from it three times.

(4) Libations of water and the recital of chapter twelve, the Zoroastrian creed beginning with the execration of the demons. Libation of *jivam*. A single *barsom* twig is placed on the *jivam* cup. Washing of the mortar, etc. Chapters thirteen to eighteen are made up of invocations and dedications of sacred objects.

(5) Chapters nineteen to twenty-one, forming the *Bagan yasht*, praise and comment on the three main prayers, i.e., the *Yatha ahu vairyo*, the *Ashem vohu*, and the *Yenhe hatam*. The *barsom* twig on the *jivam* cup is brought into contact with the *barsom* tie.

(6) The same rite goes on during chapter twenty-two, a prelude to the Second Preparation of the haoma, which lasts from chapter twenty-five to chapter twenty-seven. The juice is squeezed and strained but will not be drunk by the *zot* in the course of this yasna. Chapter twenty-three invokes the Fravashis (souls of the deceased) and is part of the *Srosh darun* (above, no. 2). In chapter twenty-seven there is a precise agreement between gesture and text when the *zot* strikes the sides of the mortar with the pestle.

(7) From chapter twenty-eight on, while the mortar is

struck again, the haoma filtered and poured, and the mortar and haoma cup put upside down, the Gathas are recited, the most sacred texts of the whole liturgy. Their order of recitation recalls the unfolding of the history of the world, from beginning (alluded to in the *Ahuna vairya,* Yasna 27) to end (with which the *Airyema ishyo,* Yasna 54 is concerned). Chapter fifty-five praises the Gathas and another group of texts called Stot-yasn but hard to identify. The bulk of the ceremony is over. The rest is but a sort of deconsecration[22] or desacralization. The implements are put back in their places.

(8) Chapters fifty-six and fifty-seven are to the glory of Srosh.

(9) Chapter fifty-eight contains the prayer *fshusha.* Chapter fifty-nine is largely repetitive. Chapter sixty is another famous prayer, the blessing of the house of the just; chapter sixty-one invokes the efficiency of the chief prayers.

(10) The correspondence between gestures and words begins again, with less precision, and lasts a few chapters. The two priests, as they pronounce chapter sixty-two in praise of the Fire, *Atash Nyaish,* perform certain gestures while looking at the fire, presenting it with the haoma, etc.

(11) During the recital of chapter sixty-three to sixty-nine, pertaining to water and its consecration, *ab zohr,* the water is mixed with haoma, with *jivam,* is poured on the *barsom,* etc.

(12) The last three chapters invoke the Deities and praise Ohrmazd's good creation. In order to complete the Yasna, the only remaining act is to pour the sacred water back into the well.

22 Drower, "The role of Fire," p. 75.

Such is the principal ceremony of the Parsee cult. Performed before the sacred fire and addressing, through it, Ohrmazd and various deities, it is executed by one or more pairs of priests for the sake of the faithful who pay for it or for the sake of those for whom they pay, but the faithful never attend it in a crowd. It is strictly forbidden to the unfaithful.

THE HAOMA

The haoma is not only a plant and a liquor, it is also a god. Sacrifices were offered to him and certain parts of the victim, as we have seen, were reserved for him. Being a god, he is killed as he is pounded. The Brahmanas tell the same thing of Soma: "For Soma is a god and they kill him in that they press him" (Shatapatha 3.9.4.17). The sacrifice of Haoma is therefore that of a dying god offered to a god. If one recalls that, after the offering, the priest and the faithful swallow the victim and, by so doing, partake in the god's immortality, it will be recognized, following Zaehner,[23] that this conception strikingly resembles the Catholic mass. It is necessary to correct this impression immediately by observing that the two religions differ in the importance they give to this ideology. What is the very center of the Christian liturgy is barely surmised in the Mazdean ritual—which cannot allude to a historical fact such as the crucifixion of Jesus.

If one studies in the texts and the gestures the value given to the haoma sacrifice, and more generally to the Yasna as a whole, one comes to the conclusion that it is a life-giving operation, analogous to the soma sacrifice in India. One of the

[23] *Encyclopaedia of Living Faiths* (1959), p. 222.

aspects of its action is revealed in procreation. The heroes
who first pressed the haoma—according to the *Hom Yasht*—
always obtained, as sole favor, an offspring. For the same
reason Zurvan offered sacrifice during a thousand years and
in India Prajapati offers ghee to the fire.[24] And as Prajapati's
most eager adversary is Mrtyu, "Death,"[25] so is Haoma the
enemy of the daevas and death. Haoma was until recently
given to the dying as a viaticum, the aliment of immortality.
In the same fashion, the Vedic bards who have drunk the
soma are immortal; and, according to the Brahmanas (S.
Lévi, p. 88), the sacrifice raises the sacrificer up to the celestial
world.

The struggle against the daevas is carried on particularly by
striking the mortar with the pestle: so in India (according
to the Maitr. 4.8.1), "Manu had vases; if they were clinked,
all the Asuras on that day ceased to exist." But another significance is added later on in the Dabistan. According to this
book, the sound of the pestle has an eschatological value:
it recalls—or anticipates—the thoughts, words, and deeds
that will take place on the coming of the Savior.

The life-giving power is manifest at every stage of the
Yasna. We have noted the bringing together, in the same rite,
of water, *barsom*, and the crescent-shaped stands. The same
is true for the branch of pomegranate, a commonplace
fecundity symbol, and milk, called precisely *jivam*, or "living." Here is, moreover, how the Datastan i Denik interprets
the rite of pouring water three times into the haoma mortar:
it shows the world the evaporation, formation, and fall of
rain. In the case of the moon crescent, a confusion has crept

---

[24] Taitt. Brahmana 2.12.1–3.
[25] Sylvain Lévi, *La doctrine du sacrifice*, pp. 18 ff.

in between its "natural" and its "social" value. Modi writes (p. 262) that the moon and her crescent give an idea of increase or growth. But according to Datastan i Denik 48.17, the crescent is used there as a royal emblem. Undoubtedly fire is king and, on the other hand, the crescent is conspicuous in the iconography of the Sassanid kings: hence arose this interpretation by the Datastan.

The Yasna is most often performed for the sake of the deceased—for an obvious reason. And it is to the deceased in particular that the offering of the *darun* (bread) and *goshhudo* (ghee) is destined, a rite which, as we have seen, can constitute a special ceremony, in that case addressed to Srosh, conductor of the dead souls. The desacralization with which the Yasna ends (after the recital of the Gathas) and in which water plays an important role, no longer of fecundation but rather of purification, has for its Indian counterpart the *avabhrtha*, the final cleansing. We are therefore fully justified in comparing the haoma rite with the soma rite and in seeking a common original meaning for them, as Victor Henry did in an appendix, "Esquisse d'une liturgie indo-eranienne," to Caland's *Agnistoma*. Here are its main points:

(1) It is certainly a communion-sacrifice, both between the faithful and with the being present in the liquid, who in both speculations has become a god. It is easily conceived that the beverage was originally drunk by the entire community but later restricted to the sacerdotal class, once it had developed. But the Indo-Europeans were not totemists.

(2) The god must be propitiated by our gifts so that he will in turn reward us with his; and he must be strengthened, his ardor stimulated with a view to his performing beneficent feats (cf. Yasht 8.24).

(3) One reads in the Rig Veda (9.108.10 addressed to Soma): "Clarify thyself into rain from the sky." The identification of soma and rain may have taken place through various associations of ideas, traces of which should be easy to recover from the Avestan mythology.

Concerning the difference in the preparation of the liquor, with a mortar for the haoma but with a millstone for the soma, Henry notes that the latter is an innovation as against the mortar (still mentioned in the Veda), to suit the needs of multiple libations or of the drinking by an increasing number of officiants.

Comparison between Vedic and Avestan officiants also reveals a general analogy. Before being reduced to two, the number of the Mazdean priests was eight: they are still named in the Visprat. If on either side the dumb or semi-dumb supervisor is subtracted (*sraoshavarez* and *brahman*), there remains in Iran the *zaotar* and six others, in India "the seven *hotr*," i.e., the *hotr* and the six others. But it seems impossible to make all their names coincide one to another. Only the functions correspond, and they only partially. To the *potr* ("filterer") would correspond the *asnatar* who washed and filtered the haoma; to the *nestr,* the *frabaretar* who brought the vases and divers implements and the *aberet* who drew water. In conclusion, only the role of the *zhautar* is securely attested for the Indo-Iranian period.

These remarks of Victor Henry should be supplemented by an observation on the disposition of the sacrifice. In the setting of the Yasna, as well as in the location of the Vedic rite, figurations of the sun, moon, and earth are easily recognized. Fire is a rival or substitute of the sun: that is probably why it is placed on a circular vase. The moon is present in the form of the two metal crescents on which the *barsom* is repeatedly placed—a fecundity rite. As for the earth, it is the table, necessarily square (as the earth was supposed to be), in front of which the chief priest sits. This cosmic symbolism is also attested in some details: the *darun,* according to the Pahlavi Rivayat 56.1, is arranged like the world; it is round like the world, etc.[26]

The Parsee priests, when sacrificing, turn preferably to the south. The Hindu priests, on the contrary, avoid facing south. How do we explain this difference? One might think at first that India, a tropical country, dreads above all heat, and hence the south; whereas Iran, more northerly, has no greater enemy than cold, in the north. However, if one looks at the alleged motives, on either side, another reason appears. The Hindus avoid the south as being the side of the manes or spirits of the dead. This implies, if one takes into account the well-known opposition between manes (*pitarah*) and gods (*devah*), that the north is the side of the latter. Hence it is natural that the Zoroastrians, who repudiated the cult of the ancient gods, the daevas, should have turned their back on them. It is from the north that the *Druj* of the Dead is supposed to come (Videvdat 7.2).

Never is the position and orientation of the two priests a matter of indifference. It seems that this completes the cosmic definition of a ceremony in which all the elements take part: fire, water, vegetable and (in a state of weak survival) animal nature, and in which the sun, moon, and earth are symbolically present. The entire universe, as one may infer, is brought

[26] Marian Molé, *Culte, Mythe et Cosmologie dans l'Iran ancien* (1963), p. 120 ff.

into play to avert the demons and death. The importance of orientation is attested in an inscription of Xerxes in which the Achaemenid king states that when he extirpated a cult of the daivas he ordered Ahura Mazda to be worshipped "facing Arta-wards during prayer."[27]

The Yasna came to have an Apocalyptic significance. For instance Manushcihr writes in his Datastan i Denik, Question 37.16, that "the fine-grown Haoma in its pure metal container, [which is] the glorious earthly Hoama blessed by Zarathushtra, is the symbol of that white Haoma [called] Gokaren from which [springs] the immortality [that sets in] at the final Rehabilitation [of all things]." Similarly, Zatspram states (chapter 35.15) that the sacrifice instituted by Zarathushtra is a "substitute" for the one that will take place at the final Rehabilitation: "The haoma substitutes the life-giving haoma, i.e., the white haoma which is contained in the seas and will resurrect the dead and give immortality to the living; the milk substitutes that of the cow Hadayosh who is kept in a bronze fortress watched by Gopatshah; the fire substitutes the great fire which maintains the life of the animate beings; the sacrifice substitutes the sacrifice and worship at the Rehabilitation of good." But this eschatological symbolism must be secondary, despite Molé's contention to the contrary. Otherwise how could it be explained that the Gathas are twice interrupted with texts foreign to them? We can add that the comparison we have sketched with the analogous rites in India does not point to an apocalyptic meaning. The traditional opinion must therefore be upheld: given the Yasna, seasonal

[27] In the interpretation proposed in *Bull. Sch. Orient. and Afr. Stud.* (1962), pp. 336–337. But see now R. Schmitt, *Orientalia* (1963), p. 437 ff.

or apocalyptic values or allusions were secondarily (which does not mean recently) introduced into it.

A cosmogonic interpretation is attested (Bundahishn 3.20): before the Aggressor came up, it was always midday. At midday, Ohrmazd and the Amahraspands fashioned the idea of sacrifice. In the performance of sacrifice, the whole creation was created, or rather "Creation was completed."

III
Emblems and Insignia

THE GODS

Prehistory

The prehistoric objects give little information on the religion of Iran. The chief group is that of cult figurines, most of which represent a goddess of fecundity.[1] Then come symbolic representations of rain on the admirable ceramics of Susa, Nehavend, etc., in the form of the "heavenly comb," i.e., the body of a female quadruped, more or less stylized, from which a curtain of rain falls like a gush of milk.[2]

A special category of objects is made up of the Luristan bronzes; the Mesopotamian art of animal representation seems reflected in them, but it is not known to what people or time they belonged, between the two extremes of 2,500 and 550 B.C.[3]

Two of these objects are exceptionally interesting. The

[1] Phyllis Ackermann, *Survey of Persian Art,* I, 195 ff.
[2] Lommel-Weyersberg, "Regenkamm und Himmelsrind," *Paideuma* (1939), p. 120 ff.
[3] R. Dussaud, *Survey of Persian Art,* I, 254 ff.

first is a plaque in the Metropolitan Museum, studied by Dussaud and Dumézil.[4] It seems, according to Dumézil, to illustrate the series of "para-Indian" gods enumerated in the treaty concluded in the fourteenth century B.C. between the king of Mitani and the Hittite emperor. The other is the Cincinnati Museum plaque we have already mentioned, in which, according to Ghirshman,[5] Zurvan is represented: a winged androgynous god giving birth to twins—who issue forth from his shoulders—and receive the *barsom* from three processions representing the three ages of man.

The Achaemenids.

A frequent motif in the iconography of the Achaemenids is inherited from older civilizations of western Asia. It comes in the last resort from Egypt, through the Hittites, Mitanians, and Assyrians, as has been demonstrated, after the Belgian Goblet d'Alviella and with the help of new evidence, by H. Frankfort (in his book *Cylinder-Seals*, 1939).[6] Now this winged disk may have carried along other motifs of the traditional iconography, such as the Tree of Life, eminently characteristic of the god Assur.

Erich Schmidt, in the second volume of his monumental *Persepolis* (Chicago, 1957), has made known a quantity of Achaemenid seals and imprints, the figuration of which has not yet been studied exhaustively. One point is well established: the relevance of several of these seals to Mazdean

---

[4] Dussaud, "Anciens bronzes du Luristan et cultes iraniens," *Syria*, XXVI, 196 ff.; Dumézil, "Dieux cassites et védiques," *Revue hittite et asianique*, (1950), p. 18 ff.

[5] *Artibus Asiae*, (1958), p. 37 ff.

[6] See also Bossert, "Meine Sonne," in *Analecta Orientalia* (1957).

religion. This is proved, in the case of seal 20, by the combination in one scene of the fire altar, the haoma mortar (similar to those which have been retrieved in fragments), the "Magus" and the winged disc hovering above; in the case of seal 23, by the battlements on a "fire-tower" between two personages and underneath the winged disc again.[7] The latter represents Ahura Mazda,[8] as indeed on the great reliefs of Persepolis and Behistun, and we may conclude that it does so likewise on the other seals of the same series on which it is found. Seals 18 and 19 are especially interesting for us in that the disc is supported there, respectively, by two horsemen and two winged, two-faced bull-men. (Figs. 2 and 2a.)

It would admittedly be imprudent to interpret each detail in the whole series of seals by reference to the Mazdean religion. A motif such as the hero conquering two more or less fantastic animals is not specifically Mazdean. We must therefore study all these seals, notably seals 18 and 19, without bias in order to determine the exact part of Mazdaism in them.

The motif of the sky supported by personages with their arms uplifted, elbows wide apart, also belongs to the banal iconography. It is found on Hittite reliefs, notably on the hematite seal in Dresden;[9] at Tell-Halaf;[10] in Middle As-

---

[7] A similar seal was known; *Survey of Persian Art*, IV, 123 f.

[8] Only the Parsees may still entertain doubts on this identification. Their sole argument is that the great god Ahura Mazda cannot be represented. But they cannot but admit that he was represented on Sassanid reliefs, and already on Kushan coins—as will be seen further on. Nothing, therefore, prevents us from admitting that it was he, the sky-god, who succeeded the god Assur of the Assyrian figurations, as shown by Frankfort.

[9] L. Messerschmidt, Corp. *Inscr. Hett.*, XLIII (1900), 4; Bossert, *Janus und der Mann mit der Adler- oder Greifenmaske* (1959), fig 8.

[10] Oppenheim, *Tell-Halaf*, pl 8B; Pritchard, *The ancient Near-East in Pictures* (1954), p. 653.

syrian[11] and Assyrian[12] art. It is from there that it passed to the Achaemenids.[13]

These scenes seem to illustrate a myth such as that of Atlas or, more generally, a myth of separation of heaven and earth, such as was seen in Egypt in the scene of the god Nut supporting a naked woman who arches over him and represents the vault of the celestial sky.

Who are these Atlas beings? Will the characters they have in common, their frequent animal parts and wings, allow us to identify them? A priori, what gods, demons or genii can best be entrusted with the task of upholding the sky, if not gods, demons, and genii of the atmosphere, of the air, of the winds? Indeed, the clue seems provided by the Egyptian myth in which the Atlas-god is precisely Su, the god of air. In this way the wings and bird-head are immediately explained.[14]

The other frequent feature, the animal parts, is less immediately intelligible. Why should sphinxes[15] or bull-men[16] uphold the sky? In order to account for them, it may suffice to think of the constant association of the atmospheric gods with animals. For instance, in India Indra and the Maruts, in Iran Verethraghna are incarnated in animals or compared to animals.[17] As for the bulls in particular, I wonder if, given

[11] Frankfort, *Cylinder-Seals,* fig. 57; Edith Porada, *Corpus of ancient Near-Eastern Seals in American Collections,* 690 E.

[12] Frankfort, XXXIII, b, e; Porada, 771 E.

[13] Porada, 817; *Survey of Persian Art,* IV, 124, v; Dieulafoy, *L'Art antique de la Perse,* fig. 251; and our Persepolis seals 18 and 19. An unpublished seal in the Metropolitan Museum is of uncertain attribution.

[14] Wings, griffins: Frankfort, 57; winged sphinxes: Porada, 817; Dieulafoy, 251; *Persepolis,* II, 19. Bird-head: Dresden seal, Frankfort, 57; Porada, 818 (birds).

[15] Porada, 817; Dieulafoy, 251.

[16] Pritchard, 653; Porada, 771 E; *Persepolis,* II, 19.

[17] Lommel, *Der arische Kriegsgott* (1939), p. 74; Dumézil, *Rev. Hit. et Asian.* (1950), p. 24 ff.

the context, they should not be interpreted as representing the thunderstorm with their bellowing.[18] One also thinks of Zeus, whose animal metamorphoses might be linked up with his character as a storm god.

We can now attempt an interpretation of seals 18 and 19 along the line indicated above. To begin with seal 19, what does the two-faced bull-man mean? Dicephalism is in itself susceptible of different explanations. It is frequent in the iconography of western Asia. It belongs as an essential characteristic to the Sumerian god Isimu, in Akkadian Usmu, Hittite Izzummi, minister to the god Ea to whom he introduces several personages, notably the bird-man, etc. It has been attempted, on the evidence of certain texts, to multiply the two-headed or two-faced Babylonian gods by attributing this feature to Marduk, Assur, Nimurta, Shamash, Enlil, and Tiamat. But Furlani has shown, in "Dei e demoni bifronti e bicefali dell'Asia occidentale antica",[19] that we have to do either with twin homonymous constellations, or with manners of speaking, notably an idiom putting the word "head" in the dual case by analogy of parts of the body which go by pairs. True dicephalism would then be found, apart from the god Isimu, only with certain demons with an animal body, either Babylonian or Syro-Hittite or Cypriot. Be that as it may, the frequency must be noted with which dicephalism is associated with certain animal features; the association of Isimu himself with animals is also remarkable and has been

---

[18] It will also be noted that the bull-men, although they generally have only four limbs, sometimes also have two arms attached to their human bust—thus on the Persepolis seal 36—which makes us think of the centaurs. Now the latter, even if they are separated from the Indian gandharvas, have clear atmospheric connections, if only by their birth from a cloud.

[19] *Analecta Orientalia* (1935), pp. 136 ff.

recently studied by Bossert in his *Janus und der Mann mit der Adler- oder Greifenmaske* (Istanbul, 1959),[20] where he says among other things: "It cannot be a mere chance that eagle-men or griffin-men appear on numerous monuments showing also Janus."

These associations bring us back to the atmospheric character of the sky-upholding beings. And we can surmise that it is as genii of the atmosphere, the wind, or the storm that our bull-men on seal 19 have two faces. Several facts confirm this hypothesis. In Greece we have on a Chiusi red-figured vase,[21] a two-faced Boreas. A seventeenth-century design also represents with two faces the ancient wind god of the Old Prussians.[22] Finally, in Iran the god Vayu was double. Admittedly no text, no image tells us explicitly that he had two heads, but must we not suppose that this is so when we read in the Avesta (Yasht 15.5 and elsewhere) that one part only of Vayu belongs to the Beneficent Spirit (the other to the Destructive Spirit)? Must he not therefore have two mouths, two faces? The fission later on became total, and there is in the Pahlavi books a good Vay and a bad Vay.

Apart from this particular development, what can dicephalism represent in a wind god if not rapidity, quasi-ubiquity, suggested by simultaneously pointing where he goes and

[20] *Nederlands histor.-archaeol. Inst. in het nabije Oosten.* The author is surprised at the fact that Furuza Kinal, in a paper "Ist die Herkunft des Janus Mesopotamien?" read to the Istanbul Congress in 1951, ignores the tricephalous god of Mohenjo-daro. But he himself seems to have overlooked Pettazzoni's rich studies, at least one of which, *l'Onniscienza di Dio*, had appeared when he was writing.

[21] *Annali dell'Istituto* (1860), tav. d'agg. LM; cited in Pettazzoni, *L'Onniscienza di Dio*, p. 232 ff., with the interpretations of Stark (1860) and Stephani (1871).

[22] P. Sarasin, *Helios und Keraunos* (Innsbruck, 1924), p. 169; cited in Pettazzoni, *L'Essere supremo nelle religioni primitive*, fig. 27.

where he comes from? This interpretation of seal 19 carries with it that of seal 18, in which the Atlas-horsemen remind us of a passage in the Gathas where the memory of a myth of separation of heaven and earth seems to linger on (Yasna 44.4):

Who set the Earth in its place below, and the sky of the clouds, that it shall not fall?
Who the waters and the plants?
Who yoked the two steeds to wind and clouds?

The figuration of Ahura Mazda as a winged disc, current at Behistun and Persepolis, may have been borrowed either from the Assyrians through the Parsua or the Medes, or from the Babylonians, although we have in Babylon not a single image of Marduk so represented—but this may be due to the scarcity of our Babylonian material.[23] In any event these representations on Achaemenid seals offer several remarkable traits. Sometimes the bust tops the winged disc,[24] as it does on the great reliefs of Behistun, Naqsh-i-Rustam, and Persepolis, once with a second pair of wings (123 B). But in three instances the bust seems to have come down from its flying contraption and to stand underneath, either in two pairs of wings (123 D), or in a sort of ring (123 K; 124, left-hand scene; in 124 K two different representations are juxtaposed, one with the bust on the pair of wings, the other with the bust underneath, in the ring). This ring is neither the Ecliptic[25] nor a clipeus,[26] but, as

[23] An oral suggestion of Edith Porada's.
[24] Survey of Persian Art, IV, 123 A, 124 X, right-hand scene.
[25] This is one of Phyllis Ackermann's rather arbitrary explanations, Survey of Persian Art, I, 289 ff.
[26] L'Orange, "Expressions of Cosmic Kingship in the Ancient World," in La Regalità sacra (1959), pp. 481 ff., using a design of an Achaemenid seal with an inadequate rendering of the ring.

Alföldi and Miss Segall have rightly pointed out, the moon crescent. This is to be inferred from the swell in the lower half of the ring, clearly visible in 123 K and 124 X, and which allows us to see in this ring a variant of the crescent represented in 123 J, where it carries the divine bust and is itself supported by a giant.

In order to interpret this double figuration of Ahura Mazda as solar and lunar god, we should perhaps remember that Marduk's worshipers helped Cyrus vanquishing Nabonaid and conquering Babylon, and that Nabonaid was a worshiper and champion of Sin, an international, lunar god with sanctuaries all the way from Babylonia up to Sinai. Sin, although conquered, did not perhaps completely perish.[27] Darius may have considered Ahuramazda worthy of succeeding not only the local god, Marduk, but also this great god Sin. In this way we could explain the fact that, besides the traditional figuration as a winged disc—a clearly solar representation—that with the lunar crescent is found.

The Arsacids.

Under the Arsacids, the religion of Iran was all but submerged under Hellenistic, Semitic, and astral beliefs, symbols, and practices. In Hatra, Mesopotamia, temples have been brought to light,[28] with a bust of the Sun in bas-relief in the first and one of the Moon (Selene or Nanai) in the second. The moon figures also on another relief in the same temple, standing beside two feminine figures.

[27] Evidence has been produced by Hildegard Lewy, in *A Locust's Leg* (1962), pp. 159 ff., that Cyrus finally reconciled himself with Nabonaid.

[28] In the course of excavations commenced in 1951. See Harald Ingholt, "Parthian Sculptures from Hatra," *Memoirs Connecticut Academy* (1954).

Other symbols of the astral religion have been found, chiefly in the first temple. A statuette represents the goddess Samai ("Sky"), mentioned by Lucian *(De dea Syria, 33)*. The Semitic name of the sky lent itself to a word-play with Greek *sēmeion* ("standard, sign"); therefore the standards made up of five or six planetary discs doubly deserved their name of *sēmeia*—as signs and as figurations of the sky.

Three of these standards are represented at Hatra. Once (in the first temple), an eagle—a solar bird—stands in front of a *sēmeion* made up of a crescent, a sun-disc, a full disc, and three rings. In another case, a similar standard is flanked by Orion and his dog Sirius.[29] A third standard, with one more disc, is to be seen on a more complex relief in the first temple. Cerberus is held in leash by a Hades standing frontally in the middle of the picture, with the standard planted on his right. The axe with which he is armed (besides a long sword) recalls that of Nergal. On the other hand, his Iranian costume and, even more, two serpents and two scorpions seem to assimilate him to Ahriman. In the upper right-hand corner of the relief a statuette of Atargatis is represented, seated and holding in her hand another standard of the same type.[30] The same Hades-Nergal-Ahriman is seen once again in the first temple: on a relief of an altar in honor of a deceased, this hairy and bearded deity is seen, Parthian-clad, brandishing an axe and two snakes.

In the center or at the summit of this predominantly astral religion, the god whom inscriptions call *MRN* ("Our Lord") is apparently superior to Ball Samin ("Master of heavens"), named several times along with him. He makes up a Triad

---

[29] Relief preserved in the Istanbul Museum.
[30] A statuette of Atargatis from Hatra is in the Istanbul Museum.

with *Martan* ("Our Lady") and *Bar Marayn* ("Son of the two Lords," i.e. of the Lord and Lady). The goddesses Atargatis and Allat and the lunar god Shahru are also named with him or them.[31]

The same religion, essentially Semitic and astral, prevailed at Dura-Europos on the Middle Euphrates: an altar has been found there on which a vexillum is represented and the goddess *CHMIA* (i.e., Semaia) is invoked, in the sort of pun explained earlier. But this cosmopolitan city has also yielded a synagogue and a Mithraeum. The former is decorated with frescoes depicting episodes of the Old Testament. Professor Erwin Goodenough, the specialist in symbolism of ancient Jewish art, tried to interpret with the help of the Iranian mythology the images adorning, on one of these frescoes, the main door to a city probably representing the heavenly Jerusalem, but in Greek style.[32] Each panel of this door is divided into three registers. The upper register shows a lying ox, the middle one a naked man with two children, the lower a woman in Greek attire, holding a cornucopia. Goodenough, in a hypothesis he submitted to me orally in 1959, saw in the upper picture the primeval bull, whose sacrifice, according to the cosmogony preserved in the Bundahishn, gave birth to plants and animals; in the central picture, the god Zurvan and his twin sons Ohrmazd and Ahriman; in the lower one, the Earth, or Spandarmat, on whom the semen of the bull fell. I cannot endorse this interpretation. A priori, the fact that the figuration is repeated on both sides of the door dissuades us from attributing a narrative character to it and invites us on the contrary to interpret it in a purely symbolic, decorative

---

[31] Ingholt, *Parthian Sculptures*, pp. 28 and 47.

[32] *The Excavations at Dura Europos: Final Report*, VIII, I, "The Synagogue" (Yale, 1956), plate LVII.

way. Then the bull does not look as if destined to be sacrificed, which could easily have been intimated by garlands, as on two other pictures in the same synagogue. Further, the two children in the middle register are not twins: one is obviously older than the other. Finally, the cornucopia is never an attribute of Spandarmat. The notion must therefore be given up of Iranian myths in these paintings; we have to do with Greek symbols of abundance, without any perceptible narrative link between them.

The Mithraeum is interesting not only in itself, with its paintings representing among other things two personages with the Phrygian cap—probably Zoroaster and Hystaspes—but also as evidence of the mystery-religion which had spread through all the Roman empire (See below, 130).

Kushan Coins.

Two great changes intervened in the Kushan minting under the great King Kanishka, who reigned over eastern Iran and northwestern India towards the end of the first century A.D. The coins had been Indian in character so far. Now they become Greek, both in the legends and the gods represented: Hephaistos, Helios, Selene, as well as Nanaia (Hellenized form of the goddess Nana, of Semitic origin). This phase was short lived. It probably meant that the sovereign wanted to begin his reign with the support of the Greek element of the population. Then—as he had extended his sway to all the peoples of his empire—he could afford to assert his own religion, that of Iran. Only the script and the artistic types remain Greek; the language is Iranian and so are most of the gods, when not Hellenistic (Nana) or Indian (Shiva, Buddha, or Uma).

The change takes place before our eyes. The artistic type of Hephaistos or Helios is unchanged; the name of Hephaistos is replaced by that of Fire (in Iranian: Athsho); that of Helios yields to that of Mithra. In the same way, Nanaia becomes Nana. As for Selene, her resemblance with Nana seems to have caused her to disappear. On the other hand, new deities are introduced from the Iranian religion: Mao (the moon god), Lrooaspo (Avestan Drvaspa), Oshlagno (Verethraghna), Pharro (Xvarr, "Fortune"), Ardoxsho (Ashi vanuhi, "The good Distribution"), Oato (Vata, "Wind"), Oksho (the Oxus), and last but not least, Ooromazdo ("Ohrmazd"), or Mozdooano ("Mazda victorious"). These coins prove that Kanishka was not, as has been contended, a sort of Clovis of Buddhism. He was a tolerant king, who gave Buddha a place among the numerous deities, most of them Iranian, of his empire. The same policy is pursued under Huvishka. The same gods are represented, chiefly Mithra and Mao (the Sun and the Moon). Moreover, we witness the appearance of the Iranian god ŠAOPHOPO (Xshathra Vairya, "Desirable Dominion"), of the Shivaite deities Mahasena, Skanda Kumara, and Visakha, as well as the Hellenistic Herakles, Sarapis, *OANIN∆A* (Vanainti, "The Victorious One," translating Nike), and *PI∆H* (no doubt a blunder for *ROM*).[33]

Far-reaching conclusions have sometimes been drawn from what seemed to be a female Mithra. The name is secure; but since the type is exactly that of Ardoxsho, a woman carrying the cornucopia, we must conclude, if not, with Cumont, that it was a mere mistake of the engraver (who probably could not read), rather, with Bussagli and Gnoli, that it resulted from a

[33] Despite Göbl, *Mitteilungen der Österreichischen Numismatischen Gesselschaft*, XI (1960), 8, pp. 94 ff., who leaves Rishn unexplained.

tendency, attested elsewhere also, to unite the two deities.[34]

As for *ZEIPO* or *ZEPO* or *MEIPO*, it is, as seen by Aurel Stein, *TEIPO* (Tir, "Mercury"), not, as Göbl maintains (p. 202), Nana.

Ashaeixsho, being a masculine deity, must therefore be distinguished from Ardoxsho, despite the similarity of the names. It may be, as Aurel Stein surmised, the entity Asha Vahishta ("Best Order").[35]

We have noted that Ahura Mazda was represented on two Kushan coins. One of them is especially interesting in that it shows the god riding a two-headed horse. This gold coin, now in the Numismatic Society of America, has never been adequately studied.[35a] Cunningham, who published it in the *Numismatic Chronicle* of 1892 (p. 138), wrote the following: "I take this name (*Mozdooano*) to be the same as the Avestan *mazdaonho*, the plural of Mazdao." But why the plural? Cunningham takes it to mean the dual, designating Ahura Mazda and his opposite Anra Mainyu, which seems quite unwarranted. "Here I infer," he goes on, "that the two-headed horse may be intended to typify the two spirits of good and evil, which were inherent in the supreme creator, Ormazd." He adds in a footnote that Dr. West, the great specialist of Pahlavi, suggested *Mazdovano* ("mazda-uniting"), namely the two powers. West was certainly on the right track with his

---

[34] Cumont, *Textes et Monuments . . . Mystères de Mithra*, II, p. 187 (end of note of p. 80), followed by Göbl, *Die Munzprägung der Kusan von Vima Kadphises bis Bahram IV*, in Altheim-Stiehl, *Finanzgeschichte der Spätantike* (1957), pp. 173 ff.—Bussagli, "Royauté, guerre et fécondité (à propos d'une monnaie kushane)," *Rev. Hist. des Rel.* (1951), pp. 129 ff.

[35] Markwart, *Das erste Kapitel der Gatha ushtavaiti*, p. 49. A complete list of the legends on the Kushan coins is given in Maricq, "La grande inscription de Kanishka," *Journal Asiatique* (1958), pp. 421 ff.

[35a] See Fig. 3.

reading of the Mozdooano legend. He only missed the meaning of *vano* ("victorious"). It will be noted, in connection with
this epithet, that Kanishka himself on the great inscription
of Surx Kotal (Afghanistan) is called Oanindo ("victorious");
the name of King Vonones ought also to be remembered.

In a recent article,[36] Humbach boldly interprets *Mozdooano*
as "Vanquisher of Mazda," a hypothetical designation of
Mithra. Humbach has overlooked the fact that we have another coin, the one with the legend *Ooromazdo,* which proves
that Ohrmazd, far from being vanquished and ousted by
Mithra, as Humbach would have it, was worshiped, either
standing or on horseback. These are in fact the first representations extant of Ahura Mazda except for the solar disc, with
or without a bust, studied above. The fact that he is on horseback on one of the coins is not devoid of significance, for a
horse appears rarely on Kushan coins: in fact, in only two
other cases, each time as the steed of Lrooaspo, a deity whose
association with the horse is essential, for it is the Avestan
Drvaspa, the protectress of horses. But, in the case of Ahura
Mazda, the reason for such an association is not immediately
clear. One could think of a solar symbol, which would be
justified by the identification, in eastern Iran, of Ohrmazd
with the sun: "sun," in Khotanese saka, is *urmaysde.* Or will
the horse be put in relation to the legend of the coin and
understood as a symbol of victory? The two hypotheses do not
exclude each other, and both would account for the fact that
this is a two-headed horse.[37] If he is a solar symbol, polycephal-

[36] "Der iranische Mithra als Daiva," *Festgabe Lommel* (*Paideuma,* VII:4/6),
(1960), pp. 75 ff.
[37] A close examination of the coin, made in the company of George Miles,
the amiable and learned curator of the Numismatic Society, has convinced
us that the two heads are not due to bad stamping.

ism suits him as a symbol of omniscience: it is plausible that the steed should have taken over a characteristic trait of the deity, a trait attested with the Hittites, the Phoenicians (the four-eyed god El), and on a coin of Mallos in Cilicia.[38]

On the other hand, dicephalism may, in this instance, have a more general meaning, as it has in the case of the Indian Aditi, the heavenly cow with two heads and two sexes. This is what comparison with similar cases would suggest. There are, admittedly, none exactly comparable to our coin. At Karkemish a fantastic beast with two heads is found,[39] but one is animal, the other human. On the Hittite relief of Maltaya with a procession of gods standing on animals, two of the gods have two steeds each. But two steeds is not a two-headed steed. Similarly, on the back of an Etruscan mirror formerly in the Castellani collection in Rome,[40] Artemis is represented sitting on a stag which is entirely double—head, body, and feet—a reduplication which seems strictly useless, for the goddess visibly sits on only one beast. It seems, therefore, to be purely symbolical and probably signifies an amplification and exaltation of the customary qualities of the steed. We would thus find again the symbolism we seemed to recognize in the dicephalism of the wind: a sign of rapidity.

The two-headed steed with which Ohrmazd was occasionally provided could be interpreted along the same line, as a worthy auxiliary of a victorious master, *Mazdo vano*. It may not be irrelevant that the god appeared for the first time on horseback on a Kushan coin, that is to say, among a people of con-

[38] Pettazzoni, *L'Onniscienza divina*, pp. 164 ff., 127 ff., and fig 15; *L'Essere supremo nelle religioni primitive*, pp. 53, 206, and fig. 7.

[39] Pritchard, *The ancient Near East in pictures*, p. 644.

[40] Daremberg-Saglio, *Dictionnaire des Antiquités*, fig. 2399; cited by Ringbom, *Paradisus terrestris* (in Swedish; 1959), fig. 63.

querors coming from the steppe, and at the same time as the
Thracian riding-god appears. This takes us back, at first sight,
to the sphere of solar conceptions; for the Thracian god or
hero is a solar god or hero, and that is why, as shown by
Pettazzoni,[41] he is often represented with three faces. But a
"solar god" might be an over-simplification; for he is also a
hunter-god, a conqueror of animals.

It must be understood, on the other hand, that the horse is
not only a solar symbol; that he may have assumed, by transfer,
different significations. With the Kirgizes, according to
Radloff,[42] the primeval ox, the foundation of the universe in
the Iranian conception, has become the primeval horse. This
suggests that Ohrmazd's two-headed horse may be a distant
metamorphosis of two-headed Aditi.

The Sassanids

Ohrmazd is represented on horseback on the Sassanid reliefs,
which show him in the act of conferring the investiture on a
king, who faces him likewise on horse-back. The Naqsh-i-
Rustam relief represents Artaxsher's investiture. A trilingual
inscription, in Greek, Parthian, and Pahlavi, on the god's
horse, tells us that we have to do with Zeus-Ohrmazd. The god,
on the right, carries in his left hand a stick-shaped scepter, in
his right hand the ring with ribbons, an emblem of kingship.
He is wearing a crenellated crown. Under the feet of the royal
horse a fallen enemy is lying, probably Artaban, the last of
the Arsacids, whom Artaxsher dethroned; under the god's

[41] L'Onniscienza di Dio, p. 259.
[42] Proben der Volkslitteratur, III, 384; cited in Bauman, Das doppelte
Geschlecht (1956), p. 260.

horse another enemy is also lying, no doubt Ahriman, bare-headed, his hair and beard dishevelled, with snake heads visible amidst the curls.

The investiture of Varhran I is represented in a similar fashion. It should be noted that, since the relief stops at the horses' knees, no enemies can be seen under their feet. In fact, the figuration of Ahriman on the relief of Artaxsher's investiture is perhaps the only representation of the Demon in the Sassanid period, and almost the only one from any period. The only other representation one can mention is the Nergal-Hades-Ahriman at Hatra, and perhaps the lion-headed Aion in the Mithra mysteries, of which more further on.

A relief at Naqsh-i-Rustam represents Anahita investing King Narse with the beribboned ring. They are standing; the goddess is wearing a crenellated crown.

The enemy whom Ohrmazd and Artaxsher II trample under foot on the latter's relief of investiture at Taq-i-Bostan is not identifiable, although it may be Ahriman again. Ohrmazd, to the right, with his left foot on the enemy's head, has his left arm akimbo and hands the ring with his right hand over to Artaxsher, who likewise takes it in his right hand. Ohrmazd is wearing a crenellated crown. Behind the king, to the left of the relief, stands another figure, with his feet on a lotus flower, his two hands supporting (nearly vertically) the bundle of twigs or *barsom,* and his head haloed with rays. The modern Parsees think they can recognize Zarathushtra, and this figure is currently reproduced, sold, and honored in homes and temples as the portrait of the prophet.[43] But comparison with the monument of Antiochus of Commagene and coins

---

[43] Jackson, *Zoroaster, the Prophet of ancient Iran* (1898), pp. 288 ff.

proves that we have to do with Mithra. This figure is standing, as we have said, on a lotus. This is an Indian symbol, familiar both to Buddhism and Hinduism,[44] though its ultimate origin is probably to be sought in Egypt, where Horus, among others, was represented on the lotus flower, a symbolization of the morning sun arising from primal water.[45]

Links are missing that would enable us to retrace the route of this symbol from Egypt to India and Iran. All we can say is that Buddha was shown standing on a lotus because he had come to be conceived as a solar god, an assumption which is corroborated by the fact that the first statues of him were made, in Gandhara, in imitation of statues of Apollo, another solar god. We do not know whether Mithra on the lotus was a direct replica of Buddha or of a hypothetical Apollo on the Lotus, or—a third possibility—an even more direct borrowing from some Egyptian statue imported into Iran, as was the Harpocrates found at Taxila.[46]

Finally, the upper relief on the back wall of the cave at Taq-i-Bostan represents the investiture of King Peroz[47] by Ohrmazd in the presence of Anahita. The god, on the right, hands the king the beribboned ring with his right hand, while the king grasps it again with his right hand, his left hand holding the hilt of his sword which hangs vertically from his girdle. The goddess, to the left, recognizable by the jug of water she carries in her left hand—for she is a water goddess —also hands the king a similar ring with her right hand. She

[44] Herzfeld, *Am Tor von Asien* (1920), p. 63.
[45] Siegfried Morenz & Johannes Schubert, *Der Gott auf der Blume* (1954).
[46] S. Morenz & J. Schubert, *Der Gott auf der Blume,* p. 123 and fig. 18.
[47] Not of Khosrau II, as is still sometimes written. The identification with Peroz has been convincingly proposed by Erdmann, *Ars Islamica,* IV (1937), pp. 79 ff.

is wearing a crown adorned with two strips of pearls under a row of arcs framing palmettes. A similar representation of Anahita is found on a column capital at Taq-i-Bostan. Two more figurations of the goddess are probable, the one on a terracotta of the Arsacid period preserved in Berlin,[48] the other on a water jug from the former Stroganoff collection. The terracotta is described by Ringbom:[49] "An Arsacid terracotta relief represents Ardvi Sura standing in an aedicula. We have to do with a cult statue, for by the side of the sanctuary stands a male worshipper. . . . The goddess is wearing a high crown with a large jewel and carrying a pomegranate flower before her breast. The architectural style of the aedicula is Hellenistic and presupposes most probably a Greco-Iranian temple, perhaps in the style of the Anahita-Artemis temple whose ruins are seen in Kangavar, Media. The arrangement of the folds also shows Greek influence; but the lining of the mantle gathered in a powerful arch from the armpit to the hip is a detail of costume which becomes more and more exaggerated in the Sassanid times, whilst Greek features of style gradually disappear." The other representation is also described by Ringbom (p. 15): "We see on the Stroganoff silver vase a cult statue again. This is proved by the pedestal under the goddess. She holds a dove in her hand, has a peacock in front of her and stands under an arch decorated with birds and supported by ornate columns with *putti* as capitals."

Three other representations, in which Ringbom wants to recognize the goddess, are, to say the least, dubious. They show a woman with one breast uncovered, which does not tally with the description of Anahita in the Avesta.

[48] *Survey of Persian Art*, IV, 134 B.
[49] *Zur Ikonographie der Göttin Ardvi Sura Anahita* (Abo, 1957), p. 11.

On the reverse of Sasanian coins gods are sometimes represented giving investiture, most often over the fire altar: Ohrmazd (investing Kavat, Jamasp, and Khosrau I), Mithra (Ohrmazd I and Ohrmazd II), the former recognizable by his crenellated crown, the latter by his radiate one, and Anahita (investing Varhran II), wearing a cap with an eagle-head.[50]

Instead of the fire alter, certain coins of Khosrau II show on their reverse a woman's bust whose head is in a halo of flames. We must recognize, as Göbl suggests, Anahita. This would confirm the particular connection of this goddess with fire, emphasized by Wikander (*Feuerpriester in Kleinasien und Iran*, Lund, 1946). This type is widely spread in post-Sassanid coinage.

On the coins with a fire altar, from those of Ohrmazd II onwards, a bust is sometimes seen on the altar amidst the flames (with Varhran V and Valash it is only a head). This could be Ohrmazd. But since the latter, on the Achaemenid reliefs, always hovers *over* the fire, not *in* it, it is more likely that we have to do with the deity of fire himself, Atar. But more about this type of coins further on.

The Chariot God.

The first representation of the chariot god must be dated, it seems, from the Arsacid period—third century B.C. It appears on a ritual headgear worn by a Saka queen and was found in a tumulus at Karagodeuasc (South Russia). According to Rostovtzeff,[51] "The worship of the chariot god in the Hellenistic

---

[50] Göbl, "Investitur im sasanidischen Iran und ihre numismatische Bezeugung," *Wiener Zeitschr. f. d. Kunde des Morgenl.* (1960), pp. 36 ff.

[51] *Dura Europos and its art*, p. 63.

and Roman period in Mesopotamia and elsewhere in the Near East, whether as the supreme god or one of his manifestations, goes back to Iran and to the earliest times of its history." But Tarn[52] more prudently admits that it is difficult to distinguish here the Greek influence from the Iranian.

Several facts indicate that in the time of the Kushans and perhaps earlier, the Iranian religion had reached as far as India. The existence of a solar Mithra cult is richly attested in Sanskrit literature. According to the Bhavisyapurana, the cult of the sun was brought to India by the *magas*. These were the Magi, for they wore the *abayanga*-girdle, they claimed to be descendants of Mihira (Mithra) and one of them was called Mihiramshu, which means "ray of Mithra." A legend told that Mihira had a son called Jarasavda, a name strongly reminiscent of Zarathushtra. Besides wearing the girdle, the *magas* made use of the mouth-veil and the *barsom* and were subject to several taboos like the Magi in Iran and the Parsee priests. Of the eight companions of Mithra, two come also from Iran: Rajna (Rashnu) and Srausa (Srosh). However, the Bhavisyapurana being very late (twelfth century), its testimony does not prove any Iranian influence prior to the Parsee immigration from the eighth to the tenth centuries. But numerous sun temples are known, from Multan to Gujarat, from the fifth century onwards, either through archaeology or the Sanskrit, Chinese, and Arab authors.

The *magas* were supposed to have come from the Saka country, i.e., eastern Iran, now Seistan. Their cult ultimately merged into the Hindu sect of the Sauras (= "people of the sun"). It may well be that this process of Indianization started

---

[52] *The Greeks in Bactria and India* (1938), p. 211.

as early as the Kushan period, for in the Kushan collection of coins we have seen Iranian, Shivaite, and Buddhist elements side by side.

A statue of the Iranian sun god has been discovered in a sanctuary near Kabul.[53] Von der Osten writes: "The Iranian sun god enthroned on his chariot evinces in technique and representation all those peculiarities of the Graeco-Indian art which were to give Buddhism the outward appearance of the Bodhisattva."

The sun god on his chariot is also represented in frescoes on the vault of the niche of the 120-foot Buddha at Bamiyan (Afghanistan).[54] Rowland writes: "The paintings are entirely Sasanian in style. The massive figures of donors that alternate with figures of Buddhas on a level with the head of the great statue are the pictorial equivalents of images in the Sasanian rock-cut reliefs at Naqsh-i-Rustam and Shapur. The same massive bulk and frozen dignity that charasterize the reliefs of the Iranian kings are here translated into painting. Typically Sasanian, too, is the essentially flat, heraldic patterning of the forms that is noticeable on the enormous decoration of the ceiling of the niche representing a solar divinity in a quadriga. It is a pictorial version of the relief of Surya at Bodh Gaya. Probably we are to recognize a representation of Mithra as a symbol of the Buddha's solar character. The central figure is dressed in a mantle like that worn by Kanishka in his portrait statue at Mathura; round about are figures of the dawn goddesses costumed like Pallas Athena, and, in the upper span-

---

[53] *Mémoires de la mission française en Afghanistan* (1936). Von der Osten, *Die Welt der Perser,* pl. 111, p. 121.

[54] B. Rowland, *The Art and Architecture of India* (1953), pl. 57, p. 107.

drels of the composition, divinities of the wind. The whole is
an emblem of the sky dome over the head of the colossus."

Mithras and the Lion-headed God.

Mithras, the god of the mysteries named after him, with his
"Phrygian" cap, is undoubtedly the same god who was represented in Commagene, shaking hands with King Antiochus,
and whom an important inscription, on the same site, identified with Apollo, Helios, and Hermes. On the other hand, his
name as well as certain ritual phrases in Iranian leave no
doubt[55] that he is in fact the god Mithra of the Iranians. But
in the transformation out of which the mysteries were born,
the god received new values and became charged with new
symbols.

The reliefs and paintings have enabled us to reconstitute
several episodes in the life of Mithras on earth, from his birth
out of a rock up to his final ascension to heaven.

On December 25 the birth of Mithras Saxigenus was celebrated: he had been born from the stone as lightning comes
out of the firmament. Attending his birth stood Cautes and
Cautopates, his two companions representing the rising and
the setting sun and with whom he, as middle term (*mesites*),
formed a sort of trinity: the triple Mithras of Pseudo-Dionysos.
On the other hand, Caelus and Oceanus were also present at
the birth of Mithras Demiourgos (Mithras the creator),[56] no
doubt as initial gods who had prepared the work of the demi-

[55] Despite Wikander, whose brave attempt has been refuted by Widengren,
Stand und Aufgaben der Iranischen Religionsgeschichte (Leiden, 1955), p. 90.
[56] Vermaseren, *Corpus Inscriptionum et Monumentorum Religionis Mithriacae* (The Hague, 1956–60).

urge. And Saturn hands Mithras the knife with which he will kill the bull—a cosmogonic deed par excellence. This deed is the climax of a set of episodes. First, the bull is grazing in a meadow, or he stands on a bark (probably the moon), or lies in a house. Then, as Mithras tries to get hold of him, the animal carries him away on its back, running. Then Mithras, having mastered him, carries him off on his shoulders (Commodian compares him to Cacus). After this set of exploits, worthy of Hercules, Mithras drags the bull along into a cave, the vault of which represents the sky, and there kills him. This is the scene most often represented and can be seen in all the mithraea in the place of honor, at the high altar, so to speak. Mithra's posture, his left knee on the animal's back, whose nostrils he holds with his left hand as he stabs the flank with his right, is an imitation of the classical Greek motif of the Taurocton Nike (the bull-slaying goddess of victory), except for one particular: Mithras is seldom looking before him,[57] and most often upwards and backwards. He is apparently looking through the cave's entrance at the Sun, on whose order the sacrifice is performed. The sun and moon are pictured at the two upper corners of the reliefs; along the vault, the twelve signs of the zodiac; at the keystone, sometimes Sarapis or the lion-headed god. Cautes and Cautopates are present, as well as the raven-messenger and sometimes the rooster, which is both a solar and a Persian bird. A dog and a snake lick the blood from the wound. In most cases a scorpion seizes in his claws the testicles of the bull, whose tail most often sprouts into one or three ears of corn.

[57] So in the group in the round at Ostia (probably for an aesthetic reason), and on the Rome relief where Mithras is represented *after* the murder, standing on the slaughtered bull. Many reliefs on which Mithras seems to be looking ahead are reconstitutions with the head wrongly replaced.

In another scene Mithras is represented hunting on horse-back, armed with the bow, sometimes escorted by a lion, or by a lion and a serpent. And yet another scene shows him as he causes water to gush forth from a rock by means of an arrow, an exploit recalling less the Iranian myth of the libera-tion of waters than the story of Moses and the Horeb stone.

Several reliefs illustrate the relationship of Mithras with the sun. The latter is only identical with him in virtue of the very flexible play of syncretistic identifications. He is other-wise distinct from, and superior to him, since he orders him to kill the bull. But he elsewhere kneels before Mithras, or receives from him a knight's investiture (?); elsewhere again, the two shake hands above an altar. Most often, Mithras and the Sun share a meal. Finally Mithras ascends to heaven ac-companied by Mercury on the chariot driven by the Sun; or this chariot rolls toward the Ocean.

The Graeco-Roman gods play an important role in Mith-raic mythology. It would be an error in principle to believe that every god or every detail of the Graeco-Roman religion figured in Mithraism merely as the translation of an Iranian god or feature. When Jupiter is represented by his eagle, his thunderbolt, and his globe, no allusion to Iran should be sought there, nor when—as on many reliefs in Germany—he is surrounded by the other Olympians. Who, for instance, would be Juno's Iranian counterpart? Nor is there any coun-terpart for Saturn when he hands Jupiter the scepter and the bolt (a scene translated from Hesiod, not from the Avesta), or when he gives Mithras the sickle or the knife. Jupiter strug-gling with the giants is, at the utmost, comparable to Mithras as a hunter.

Mithraism also received a motif from the Dionysiac mysteries, for instance, in the decoration of the Ptuj altar. Similarly taken over was the Atlas myth, in two forms (at Osterburken and Neuenheim): in the second case Atlas is identified with Mithras by means of the Phrygian cap.

The myth of Phaethon, pictured on the great Dieburg relief, must reflect an eschatological role of the Iranian Mithra, and this recalls the Magian cosmology recounted by Dio of Prusa.

The lion, the crater, the serpent, and the raven could represent fire, water, earth, and air, respectively. This would lead us back, perhaps accidentally, to Herodotus' note on the Persians' veneration of the elements. But it may be that we have simply a case of the Greek doctrine of the four elements.

The numerous reliefs and statues of a god with a lion's or a man's head and a body entwined in a serpent undoubtedly represent Aion, according to an iconography which, as demonstrated by Pettazzoni,[58] was constituted in Egypt. The serpent, the signs of the zodiac, the keys to open and shut the skies to stars and souls, the four wings symbolizing the seasons or the winds characterize a great cosmic god; and the lion's head, with the serpent, recall the Aion of the magic papyri. It may be surmised, however, that thanks to the equivalences so often attested, Aion was also something more. All the lion-headed statues were placed, as far as we can judge, outside the adyton, or inner shrine. Is this not the place of an evil god?

There are among the monuments of the mysteries three or four dedications *Deo Arimanio*. Ahriman is the only Iranian

---

[58] "La figura mostruosa del Tempo nella religione mitriaca," *Antiquité classique* (1949), pp. 1 ff. Reproduced in *Essays on the History of Religions* (Leiden, 1954), pp. 183 ff.

god, besides Mithra, whose name was transmitted to the West. It is a priori probable that this was the name of the lion-headed figure, the more so as a Roman inscription (Vermaseren, *Corpus,* p. 222) speaks of a *signum Arimanium,* and to what signum could this phrase refer if not to the lion-headed statue? It is even possible that a statue at Eburacum (York) gives us both the figure and the name, if we read the inscription, with Legge and against Cumont, as follows: *Volusius Irenaeius Arimani[o] v[otum] [solvit].* What remains of the ending of *Ahriman* seems to indicate a nominative or an accusative form; but there is not a single example of *Arimanius* as a person's name. We cannot, therefore, see any reason for this name here, if not to designate the god, the very god who is represented above with this mane, his clawed feet, serpents at his girdle, wings, and keys. This demonstration seems at first sight weakened by Mary Boyce's reflection[59] that the statues in question are "not invariably horrific. The human-headed ones at Merida and Modena are calm and beautiful, and some of those with beast-heads are gentle and comely enough, for example the one from Castel Gandolfo. The horrific ones can perhaps be explained as representing Time in its menacing aspect; and it is possibly easier to accept many horrific statues of Time than one or two beautiful ones of the Devil." These pertinent remarks leave open the question, to which figures does the Arimanius of the dedications correspond. In other words, what was the *signum Arimanium?*

The lion-headed god can occupy (in the Barberini Mithraeum) the same position at the keystone as Sarapis (at Dura-Europos). This will not surprise us if we see in the lion-headed

[59] "Some reflections on Zurvanism," *Bull. Sch. Or. Afr. Stud.,* (1957), p. 316.

a figuration of Aion and remember that Aion was identified with Sarapis. But the equation leontocephalous–Sarapis is not incompatible with an identification of the lion-headed figure with Ahriman. For it is known that Sarapis was Osiris, that is, at once Helios (or Zeus) and Hades.[60] Now Hades was, as Plutarch noted (*De Iside et Osiride* 46, 47), a name of Ahriman.

In conclusion Arimanius in Mithraism, though cruel, no longer has the demonic character which was his in the dualistic system of the Iranian religion. The dedications designate him unambiguously as a god. It is no longer as a demon, but as a deity—a god of the netherworld—that he subsisted in the mysteries. By identifying himself with Sarapis, he became one with Zeus and Mithras. The human-headed figurations (at Modena and Merida, in which Vermaseren recognized Mithras) and the ones with lion heads are therefore merely two variations on the theme of the Aion-Sarapis-Zeus-Helios-Mithras-Hades-Ahriman identity, without a dualistic opposition.[61] One will seek in vain, therefore, in Mithraism for a reflection of the Iranian system, either Mazdean or Zurvanistic.

These observations provide perhaps the key to one of the moot problems of Iranism: what is the relationship between the reliefs showing Mithras as a bull-slayer and the Pahlavi texts according to which the Primordial Bull was killed by Ahriman? The opinion has been formulated in our time that the reliefs, more ancient than the datable Pahlavi texts by

---

[60] The texts speak of *Aion plutonius*. On the identification of the Sun with the three cosmic levels, or with the four elements, seasons, cardinal points, cosmic periods, cf. E. Peterson, *Heis Theos* (Göttingen, 1926), p. 248. On the chthonic character of Sarapis, *ibidem*, p. 237.

[61] However, it remains unexplained why the leontocephaluses found *in situ* are outside the adyton.

seven centuries, represent also the more ancient doctrine: Mithra was the original bull-slayer; then, following condemnation of blood sacrifice in Zoroastrianism, his role was transferred to Ahriman. But recently Gershevitch[62] has given good reasons for reverting to the older interpretation, which Cumont had adopted. In this view, the role of murderer of the Bull, primitively held by Ahriman, passed on to Mithras considered as a life-giving god.

This interpretation now seems confirmed by what has just been said of the identification of Mithras with Ahriman. For it becomes clear that, even as the relief of Mithras harvesting represents Mithras as Saturn, or those of Mithras carrying the world suggest a Mithras-Atlas, even so does Mithras the bull-slayer assume a function of Ahriman.[63]

It would be another mistake, it seems, to seek in Mithraism a supreme god situated beyond the world.[64] Jupiter-Caelus, even called *summus exsuperantissimus* (translating Greek *hypsistos*), remains a cosmic god, just as the Aion mysticism is a cosmic mysticism.[65]

[62] *The Avestan Hymn to Mithra* (Cambridge, 1959), pp. 62 ff.

[63] It can be said that in this sense Mithra contributed to a *"mögliche Beseitigung des Dualismus,"* in the words of Humbach (*Festgabe Lommel,* Frankfurt, 1960, p. 79), and that this was perhaps one reason to call him *mesites* (Plutanch *De Iside* 46). But this article by Humbach is on the whole vitiated by a misinterpretation of Mozdooano: cf. above, p. 102.

[64] Like the "Unknown Father" of the Gnostics; cf. R. Grant, *Gnosticism and early Christianity* (New York, 1959).

[65] For the former, cf. Cumont, *Archiv für Religionsw.* (1960), pp. 236 ff.; for the latter, Zepf, *ibidem* (1927), pp. 225 ff.

THE MEN

Kings

Were the kings of Iran divine? As far as the Sassanid kings are concerned, the answer is yes. Both in Greek and in Pahlavi they called themselves gods, of divine descent. Two scholars, L'Orange and Widengren, working independently and using evidence of various date, project all this back to Achaemenid times. L'Orange, in his *Studies on the Iconography of Cosmic Kingship* (Oslo, 1953), quotes Beruni on the accession of Iranian kings to the throne, in a ceremony supposed to symbolize the rising of a new sun. Now, although Beruni had in mind the Sassanid kings only, L'Orange believes that just such a scene is pictured on the Persepolis reliefs which show Darius lifted on a platform carried by his subjects—under the symbol of the sky-god.

Widengren in his paper to the Congress of the History of Religions, at Rome in 1955,[66] reconstructs the royal ideology as something invariable, inherited from Indo-Iranian times. Now, it is true that the Achaemenid kings imposed great respect on their subjects. The latter had to prostrate themselves in their presence, and if invited to share their meal, a curtain would withdraw the monarch from their profane looks. Nevertheless, Cyrus and Darius and their successors undoubtedly did not consider themselves gods. We read in their inscriptions that they are only protégés of God (Ahura Mazda), with whom they have a reciprocal relationship. They say, in effect:

---

[66] Published in *La Regalità sacra* (Leiden, 1958).

Ahura Mazda made me king; he helps me because I am a just king.

If we turn to the images, again we see that the king does not appear as a god. Darius has himself represented as a hero, a strong man, stabbing or strangling a lion. This is in accord with the inscription Naqsh-i-Rustam B, where he prides himself on being a good horseman, a good marksman, etc.

The Achaemenids simply continued in this respect the attitude that had prevailed for centuries in Mesopotamia, since the time of Hammurabi. The Mesopotamian situation has been admirably summed up by H. Schaeder in his article "Das persische Weltreich" (1941):[67] "In Sumerian times the king was priest and lieutenant of the deity on earth, sharing his knowledge and interpreting his will. It was only with the Akkadians that the idea of the inner relationship between god and king coarsened into the divinization of the king. . . . Sargon's most important successor, Naramsin, even called himself "God of Akkad." Veneration of the king as a god outlived the dynasty of Akkad and the foreign rule of the Guti that followed. It maintained itself in the time of the Sumerian Renaissance under the third dynasty of Ur. Only the leaders of the new Semitic people of the Amurrites pushed it into the background. . . .

"From Hammurabi's time (1792–1750 B.C.) on, the divinisation of the rulers (except for traces void of real significance in the titles of the kings) disappears from the history of the East, in so far as it is under the influence of Babylonian culture. The Achaemenids also know nothing of it and only in Egypt where it had long been at home and had never been given up, do they approve of its external forms."

[67] Repr. *Der Mensch in Orient und Okzident* (Munich, 1960), pp. 49 ff.

The heroic feat of the king fighting or strangling the lion is represented on the great Persepolis reliefs, as well as on seals number 123 L and 124 B of the *Survey*. Hunting scenes are sometimes depicted in a purely realistic fashion, profane in appearance (123 O, Q, R, S). The fantastic character of the sport may be noted in 123 M (where it is symmetrically duplicated, a traditional motif reminiscent of Gilgamesh's exploit); the same is true of the steed in 123 B and G, 124 C and L. Ahura Mazda's winged disc dominates the scene in 123 B and M, whereas a priest or worshiper stands in front of an altar or censer, or underneath a lunar crescent (123 C). The winged disc, with a bust of Ahura Mazda, may also hover above a realistic hunting scene in which the king on his chariot shoots arrows at a standing lion, between two palm trees (123 A). In a more fantastic vein, on the other hand, the king himself is seen as a scorpion-man, shooting a prey with his bow, under the signs of the sun and moon (123 N). The same personage, only without a crown, is at rest in 123 H, in front of a priest who raises his right hand towards him in the gesture of worship; behind him are a small quadruped and a palm tree. On another seal, the king is figured as a human-headed winged bull, similar to those seen at Persepolis (124 G). Did the duel of the king with the lion have a symbolic value? If so, the most obvious meaning would be that the king, by killing the lion, superseded him as a solar power.

Another kind of combat profusely represented on the great Persepolis reliefs is a very old traditional motif: the lion attacking a bull. This cannot be a victory of good over evil, for what in the bull is evil? It is a very old myth of the might of the sun, represented at Megiddo, Mari, Byblos, in Africa, in which the sun is symbolized now as a lion, now as a bird—

two very clear symbols—and in which the conquered animal, according to Lommel's remark,[68] is not an evil being. In any case, the size of the Persepolis reliefs with the lion and bull and their conspicuous situation invite belief that they allude to the power of the king.

It is attested for three Arsacid kings that they considered themselves gods. A beardless king, perhaps Phriapitius, calls himself *theos* on a coin; Artaban II calls himself *Theopator;* the Greeks gave Phraates IV the unofficial title of "almighty god."

Ammianus Marcellinus, noting that the Sassanids said they were brothers to the sun and moon, compares this to the divine cult with which Arsak I (the eponymous ancestor of the Arsacids) was honored, but without telling us whether he was already so worshiped during his lifetime, which is doubtful. Much more probably, the divinization of living kings seems to have been borrowed by the Arsacids from the Greek dynasts, the successors of Alexander. Among these, that custom is first attested with Antimachos (son of Euthydemos), whom his coins call a god; then with Antiochus IV, who in 175 takes the ray-surrounded crown of the god Helios and assumes in 169 the title Epiphanes, considering himself a manifestation of Zeus. This Seleucid usage, a prelude to the divinization of the Roman emperors, has often been debated. It seems to me to proceed from Alexander's own example. That is particularly clear in the case of Antiochus, who overtly considered himself as a new Alexander and restorer of his empire. However, Arsak, the ancestor of the Arsacids, was divinized, if only after his death. The testimony of Ammianus Marcellinus on

---

[68] *Der arische Kriegsgott*, p. 73 n. 1; cf. Frobenius, *Kulturgeschichte Afrikas* (1933), p. 144.

this matter is borne out by the coins. Most of the Arsacid coins show a personage with the bow, seated on the omphalus, the navel of the earth. Is he an Iranian Apollo or is he Arsak? Opinions differ, but we may quietly assert that he is both: the ancient image of Apollo seated on the omphalus, current on Seleucid coins, was taken over by their Arsacid successors to represent Arsak as a god.

The Kushan kings adopted the shoulder flames, a feature known on Babylonian cylinders, where it characterized gods—incidentally it was taken over by Buddhism in eastern Iran, to adorn the Buddha.

The Sassanid kings not only called themselves gods: they imitated gods in their attire, notably in their crown.[69] The crown in itself was a revival of an Achaemenid custom under the Sassanids, and an immediate continuation of the crown used by the princes of Persis under the Arsacids.

Artaxsher does not seem to have adopted the crown at once: on his first coins, he still wears a kind of bonnet, adorned with a star or an eagle. Only later, perhaps when he had dethroned and succeeded Artaban, did he wear—not exclusively—the crenellated crown of Ohrmazd. The crenellated crown was already in use with Hittites and Elamites, especially as a headgear for goddesses and queens. It is also found in Assyria, then again in Achaemenid art—worn by a goddess in the Oxus treasure—and is mentioned in the Avesta in the description of Anahita (Yasht 5.128). Darius wears one on the rock-relief of Behistun. In the Arsacid period, apart from the coins of

---

[69] Erdmann, "Die Entwicklung der sasanidischen Krone," *Ars Islamica*, XV–XVI (1951); Göbl, "Aufbau der Münzprägung," in Altheim-Stiehl, *Ein asiatischer Staat* (Wiesbaden, 1954), and the article quoted above on investiture.

Persis, mentioned above, it is worn only by figurations of Tyche.

Each Sassanid king had one or more crowns, all of which differed in some particular from those of his predecessors. Their type changed gradually, so that Erdmann was able to distinguish three successive groups. Originally the headgear of the Sassanid kings consisted of three parts: above, a spherical coil of hair wrapped up in a piece of fabric; then the crown proper, adorned with emblems; finally, to fasten the crown on the head, a ribbon or diadem, often adorned with one or two rows of pearls and ending in two floating ends at the back. If this diadem corresponds to the beribboned ring the gods handed to kings in token of investiture, one can assert that both objects symbolized the Xvarr or Royal Fortune. In this case the diadem would be the essential piece in the crown, which would explain why it persisted into post-Sassanid art.[70]

In the first group of crowns, up to Shapur III (whose reign ended in 388 A.D.), each crown referred to a single god. Artaxsher, Shapur I, and Shapur II had the crenellated crown of Ohrmazd; Varhran I wore the spiked crown of Mithra; Varhran II and Ohrmazd II wore the wings of the bird Varemgan, one of Varhran-Verethraghna's incarnations; Narse and Shapur II had the palmetted crown of Anahita, to whom the caps of Artaxsher and Shapur I referred, being adorned with, or shaped as, an eagle.

Thanks probably to this divine allusion not less than to the Xvarr emblem, the crown had a quasi magic power. "This significance appears most clearly," Erdmann writes (p. 87,

---

[70] Erdmann, *Die Entwicklung der Sasanidischen Krone* (1951), p. 121.

n.4), "when according to Ammianus Marcellinus Shapur in the battle for Amida wears instead of his crown, which in no circumstances, probably, could be worn outside the palace, a gilded ram's head, adorned with precious stones, which reminds us either of the animal-headed caps of many Sasanians, or of their occasional crowns with ram's horns. It must however remain an open question whether this ram helmet of Shapur referred to Verethraghna, to whose incarnations the ram belonged, or represented the Xvarr, which in the Kar Namak appeared to Artaxsher in the shape of a ram. Perhaps both conceptions were related to each other."

In the second group of crowns, from Varhran IV (388) onwards, there is no more distinction between gods: the same crown may allude to several gods; for instance, that of Varhran is crenellated, an allusion to Ohrmazd, but carries also Varhran's wings. And from the time of his successor Yazdakart I, a new god, Mah, is represented by his own emblem, the lunar crescent. Then, from Yazdakart II on, the emblems are no longer limited to the crown proper but invade the coil of hair.

In the third group, from Valash (483 A.D.) onwards, astral symbols appear on the obverse of coins, "a moon-crescent above each shoulder of the king and a star behind his head." From Khosrau II on, the spherical coil is replaced by a star; one can only wonder to what religious conception this change corresponded.

The crown eventually became so heavy that (according to the Arab historians) the Sassanid kings from Khosrau I onwards did not wear it any more; it hung above their throne. This usage passed on to the court of Byzantium, where it was observed in 1170 by Benjamin of Tudela. As for the shapes of the throne, they were perpetuated at the court of the Baghdad caliphs.[71]

Astral symbols had assumed an increasing importance towards the end of the Sassanid period. So we may explain a design such as that of the Klimova cup:[72] on a chariot drawn by four *zebus* (lunar animals) over which two Cupids hover, the king is seated on a throne entirely resting on a lunar crescent. It is known from other sources (Eutychius) that Khosrau II, who was the last important Sassanid king, had married a Christian princess and was accessible to all kinds of superstitions, surrounding himself with astrologers and sorcerers and himself practising astrology. That is probably the reason why from his time onwards the royal crown, the crenellated crown of Ohrmazd with the wings of Varhran, is surmounted by a crescent and a star.

The throne of Khosrau II also had an astral character.[73] A description of it is given by the Arab historian Tha'alibi, the Persian poet Firdousi, and the Greek historian Kedrenos. The latter told how the Byzantine emperor Heraclius—the one who recovered the "true cross" which had been carried away from Jerusalem—found in 624 in the palace of Ganzak, after the flight of Khosrau, "the horrible idol of Xosrau and his portrait enthroned in the roof of the palace which had the shape of a globe, as in heaven, with the sun, moon, and stars all around, which the idolaters worshipped as gods. And he had placed all around him messengers carrying scepters. This enemy of God had ordered machines to be made there to cause

---

[71] Erdmann, *Die Entwicklung . . .* , p. 114.

[72] Herzfeld, *Jahrb. d. Preuss. Kunstsamml.*, t. 41.

[73] The fundamental study is Herzfeld's article, "Der Thron des Xosrau," Jahrb. d. preuss. Kunstsamml., t. 41; see also Christensen, *L'Iran sous les Sassanides* (1944), pp. 466 ff.

drops to fall like rain and to produce noises like thunder."
Tha'alibi is more precise: "It was a throne made of ivory and
teak, whose plaque and balustrades were of silver and gold.
Its length was a hundred and eighty cubits. On the stairs were
seats of black wood and ebony whose frames were in gold.
This throne was surmounted with a gold and lapis-lazuli bald-
achin, where the sky and stars, the signs of the zodiac and the
seven climates were represented, as well as the kings in their
different attitudes, in banquet or in battle or hunting. There
was also a mechanism indicating the hours of the day. The
throne itself was entirely covered with four carpets in brocade
figured in gold and adorned with pearls and rubies, and each
of these carpets was especially devoted to one of the seasons."

The Iranians had a national flag, the *drafsh-i-kavyan,* which
fell into Muslim hands at the battle of Qadisiya in 636 when
the Muslims invaded Iran. The name of the flag, which meant
"flag of the Kavis," i.e. of the ancient kings, to whom the Sassanids expressly connected themselves from Kavad onwards,
was interpreted in Sassanid times by a legend: a smith named
Kavag, under the rule of the usurper Dahak, gave the signal
of revolt by hoisting his leathern apron on a lance. The tyrant
was overthrown and gave way to Freton. From then on the
flag thus improvised was the emblem of the kings of Iran. It
has been described by several Arabic and Persian authors.
According to Tabari, it was made up of panther fells and was
eight cubits by twelve. Bal'ami says the Iranians had added
jewels to it at each of their victories. It was garnished with
gold and silver coins, precious stones and pearls. Tha'alibi
says the sovereigns linked their fortune with it and rivaled
each other in increasing its splendor, so that it eventually became the marvel and wonder of the centuries. They had it

carried before them in the combats. According to Firdousi, five *mobads* or priests carried it before the marching army. According to Ibn Khaldun, a talismanic figure made up of astrological digits was brocaded on it. When the flag had fallen into Muslim hands, it was brought to Omar, "who ordered it to be severed from its pole," Tha'alibi tells us, "and to be cut into pieces and shared out among the believers."

The Sassanid monograms, signs engraved on the coins and elsewhere, have not yet given up their secret, despite the studies of Unvala and Jänichen. The latter would derive them from owners' marks that were made on horses with a red-hot iron. He recognizes in them, among other motifs, a stylized rooster. One might perhaps also look for abbreviated words.

The celebrated Hymn of the Pearl, a Syriac work preserved in the Acts of Thomas, was intensively examined by Reitzenstein[74] with respect to its symbolism. The pearl is a symbol of the soul, of the divine spark which man—in the legend the king's son—has lost and tries to recapture. Now, this tale has been assumed by Widengren[75] to be of Parthian origin, because there are in the Syriac text many Parthian loan-words. On the other hand, Wikander[76] has pointed out, in support of an Iranian origin of the Hymn of the Pearl, that in Persian the word *gohr* means both pearl, jewel, and substance, essence, and that in Firdousi's *Shahnama*, at the coronation of Khosrau, a pearl is said to come from the *Farr* (or Glory) of God. But, first, Parthian loan-words in a Syriac text are easily ac-

[74] Whose entire rich production can be said to be but a commentary on the hymn; cf. Edsman, *Le Baptême de Feu* (1940), p. 193, n. 4.
[75] "Der Iranische Hintergrund der Gnosis," in *Zeitschr. f. Religions- u. Geistesgeschichte* (1952), Heft 2.
[76] In his review of Edsman's *Baptême de Feu, Svensk Teol. Kvartalshrift* (1941), pp. 228 ff.

counted for as reflecting the general cultural contacts of Iran and Syria during the Arsacid period, not the Iranian origin of that particular text. This being so, Wikander's remarks are to be judged in the context of the wide-spread symbolism of the pearl: too many peoples share with the Persians and the Syrians a special, quasi-magical respect for the pearl to allow any deduction to be drawn concerning an Iranian origin of the Syriac legend.

Classes

The three social classes of ancient Iran, priests, warriors, husbandmen-breeders, reflecting the tripartite ideology of the Indo-Europeans, have been variously symbolized. In the Scythian legend, told by Herodotus, they are symbolized by gold objects which fall from Heaven.[77] Here is the narrative of the Greek historian: "The first man who appeared in their country which had hitherto been desert was called Targitaos, who was said to be a son of Zeus and of a daughter of the river Borysthenes. He had himself three sons, Lipoxais, Arpoxais, and lastly Kolaxais. In their lifetime objects of gold fell from the sky onto the land of Scythia: a plough, a yoke, an axe, a cup. When he saw these objects the eldest hastened to take them, but when he arrived, the gold began to burn him. He drew back and the second came forth, without better success. The first two having given up the burning gold, the third brother came up and the gold went out of its own accord. He took possession of it, and his two brothers, convinced by this sign, surrendered the kingship to their junior."

[77] Dumézil, *L'idéologie tripartie des Indo-Européens* (Bruxelles, 1958), pp. 9 ff.

"It is clear," Dumézil writes (p. 10), "that these four objects refer to the three social activities of the Indians and 'Iranians of Iran'; the plough with the yoke evokes agriculture; the axe was, with the bow, the national weapon of the Scythians; and other Scythian traditions preserved by Herodotus, as well as analogous well-known Indo-Iranian facts, invite us to see in the cup the instrument and symbol of cult offerings and sacred carouses."

According to another piece of symbolism, going back to Indo-European times like the ideology itself,[78] each function or class was represented by a color: white for priests, red or versicolor for the warriors, dark blue for the husbandmen-breeders. References to the white color of the priestly attire are numerous and will be taken up again below. One reads in the Mihr Yasht, 126,[79] that "on the left of the god flies the libation-bearing, truth-owning goddess Razishta Cista, white, dressed in white garments, the likeness of the Mazdayasnian religion."

On the three colors, the important text is Bundahishn 3, telling how Creation was made for the struggle against the forces of evil. Here are paragraphs 4 to 6:[80]

"Ohrmazd himself donned a white garment and it had the stamp of priesthood: for wisdom is ever with the priests who are guides to men, etc.

"Vay, the good one, donned a garment of gold and silver, adorned with precious stones, purple, and having many colors, and it had the stamp of warriorhood; for he pursues the enemy

---

[78] Dumézil, pp. 25 ff. and 98.
[79] In the translation of Gershevitch, *The Avestan Hymn to Mithra* (Cambridge, 1959), p. 137.
[80] Zaehner, *Zurvan* (Oxford, 1955), p. 333.

from behind that he may smite the Aggressor and protect creation. . . .

"From time the firmament (Spihr) was fashioned, the body of Zurvan of the long Dominion, the good destiny of the gods [the signs of the Zodiac]: he donned a dark blue garment and it had the stamp of the husbandmen; for its office is to rule the destinies of the world aright even as that of the husbandmen is to till the soil and to deliver us its produce in due course."

In a study which is more original than it is convincing, Widengren[81] has tried to prove the existence of fraternities chiefly recruited in the third class and being a counterpart to the *Männerbünde* (belonging to the second function) which Wikander had postulated.[82]

The Degrees of Initiation to the Mysteries of Mithras

We know through St. Jerome and a quantity of monuments what were the degrees of initiation, with the characteristics and symbols of each.[83] Beginning with the lowest: Corax (crow or raven), Nymphus (bridegroom), and Miles (soldier) constituted the three inferior degrees, at the service of the other four; these were called Leo (lion), Perses (Persian), Heliodromus (course of the sun), and Pater (father). Each of the degrees was under the protection of a planet; and each

---

[81] Harlekintracht und Mönchkutte, Clownhut und Derwischmütze," *Orientalia Suecana* (1953), pp. 41 ff. By the same scholar, "Some remarks on riding costume and articles of dress among Iranian peoples in Antiquity," *Arctica* (1956), p. 228.

[82] *Der Arische Männerbund* (Lund, 1938).

[83] Vermaseren, *Corpus Inscriptionum et Monumentorum Religionis Mithriacae*, 2 vols. (The Hague, 1956–1960); *Mithras, de geheimzinnige God* (Amsterdam, 1959).

had a particular relationship with Mithras. The strong pro-
portion of Greek terms in the list will be noted: only Miles
and Leo are Latin—which is immediately understandable in
the case of the former, since the initiates are, most of them,
soldiers in the service of the Roman state. Pater is ambiguous.
The Corax or raven is the messenger—this is why he is under
the protection of Mercury—who orders Mithras to kill the
bull. The initiates of this rank sometimes wore a raven mask.
The Nymphus or bridegroom is, as such, protected by Venus.
He unites himself in a mystical marriage with Mithras, represented by the Pater. His symbols are the nuptial torch, the
crown (also nuptial), and the lamp, representing the new
light provided by union with that god. The Miles or soldier,
under the protection of Mars, is initiated in a ceremony in
which he is presented, at the point of his sword, with a crown
which he refuses, saying: Mithras only is my crown.

The Leo or lion symbolizes fire and must avoid contact
with water; this is why he purifies himself not with water but
honey.[84] He can wear a lion mask. He is under the protection
of Jupiter. Fire unites him to Mithras and the sun; but the
lion-head suggests the leontocephalous Aion of the magic
manuscripts. The Perses or Persian is protected by the moon.
He also rubs himself with honey, but that is, according to
Porphyry, because that substance has a preserving propriety:
like the moon, the Perses "preserves" the fruit. On the other
hand, he has among his attributes Saturn's sickle: this is a
way of identifying himself with Mithras, for the latter is
represented (at Dieburg) as a harvester, i.e., as a "new Saturn,"
the king of a new Golden Age. The Heliodromus is under

[84] Cf. Edsman, *Ignis divinus* (Lund, 1949), pp. 219 ff.

the protection of the sun, whose daily course he represents. His emblems are the whip (for the solar team), the radiate crown, the torch, the globe, the nimbus. He is represented saluting the Pater, a substitute of Mithras, whilst in front of them Mithras and the Sun share a ritual meal. The Pater is under the protection of Saturn, the highest of the planets and in a sense the supreme god. He is also, as we have seen, the personification of Mithras (who, we have also seen, was a new Saturn): therefore he wears the Phrygian cap and carries the sickle. The Pater is the chief of a community, but there seems to have been, inside that degree, various hierarchic grades, *antipatros* at Dura, *pater sacrorum* and *pater patrum* in Rome.

IV

The Human Projection

IN THE BELIEFS

Zoroastrian dogmas and ritual provide the means to express, in word and deed, man's relationship with God and the world. As Denkart 321.34 has it, "all creatures are mirrored in man, who is the symbol of Ohrmazd." Each of the two parts of this formula is found elsewhere in more detail, and there is also, of course, the direct connection between God and the world. God is said to have carried in himself, like a mother her child, the *menok* (spiritual) state of the world (Great Bundahishn 16.10–11). In a passage preserved by the Arabian author Jayhani (see Menasce, *Donum . . . Nyberg*, 1954, p. 52) Ohrmazd says, "I have created the whole world from myself: the souls of the just from the hair of my head, the skies from my brains . . . the sun from my eyes, etc."

In a more elaborate fashion, the creation of the world is said to have proceeded in successive stages, one of which is a Cosmic Man. This doctrine has been somewhat obscured by the difficulty of interpreting a certain term, *asrok karp,* designating the intermediate stage between "Infinite Light" and "all the creatures." But I think it may be shown—as I have tried to do in *East and West* (1962) and in the *Unvala Memorial Volume* (1964)—that *asrok karp* meant "a form of fire," elsewhere designated as *ataxsh karp*.

From this form of fire, which was "bright, white, round, and manifest afar," all creatures were made. We learn more about this form from Manushcihr who tells us in his Datastan-i-Denik, Question 63, that its name was Ohrmazd: *ke-sh 'nam*[1] *'an i Ohrmazd but*. This name may cause surprise, for what could be the meaning of Ohrmazd creating a form called Ohrmazd? All becomes clear, however, if we remember that in Manichaeism Ohrmizd was the name of Cosmic Man. The original myth seems therefore to have told how Zurvan created a spherical body of fire called Ohrmazd.

Be that as it may, Manushcihr goes on to say that within this form of fire God "created the entity called Man." And this was Gayomart, the Primeval Man. And according to Great Bundahishn 21.6, Gayomart was as broad as he was high, which can hardly mean anything but that he was spherical. In this he imitated, so to speak, the sphericity of the "form of fire."

The whole picture is paralleled in Greek thought, for according to Aristophanes in Plato's *Symposium*, primeval man was spherical and this was not a poet's fantasy but, as Ziegler has shown,[2] it is an application to man of the Orphic theory of the origin of the world. Since the world was originally spherical—the cosmic egg—so must have been man. This

---

[1] Zaehner's reading, *Bull. Sch. Orient, and Afr. Stud.* (1959), p. 367, *dam* = "creature" instead of *shem* = "name," gives a less satisfactory sense.

[2] Menschen- und Weltenwerden,' *Neue Jahrbücher für das Klassische Altertum,* 1913, 529.

picture expresses a tendency characteristic of Greek thinking
in the middle of the fifth century, namely, that of explaining
man in terms of physics—a sort of anthropomorphism in reverse. For instance, Empedocles not only equates in a rather
banal way man's hair with leaves and birds' feathers, but says
that "we see Earth by means of Earth, Water by means of
Water, divine Air by means of Air," etc. And the same principle, witness Plato in *Phaedrus* 270c, is the very base of Hippocratic medicine: it is not possible, Plato thinks, to compre-
hend the nature of the soul without that of the universe, nor
can we even, if we are to believe Hippocrates, speak of the
body without this method.

In the Hippocratic Corpus the man-world correspondence
is illustrated several times: not only in the *Peri Hebdomadon*,
but in the *Peri Diaites* and other similar texts. And this brings
us back to Iran, with the long passage in Great Bundahishn
189.3ff., where it is shown how "the body of man is a *handa-
cak*," i.e., a measure, of the world. We shall not fail to be
reminded of Protagoras' celebrated sentence, that Man is
the measure of all things. Since this sentence, diversely interpreted, was often quoted throughout Antiquity, from Plato
through Xenophon and Aristotle to Plutarch, it may very
well have been known to the Iranians.[3] And since the notion
of a spherical universe probably originated in Babylonia and
passed from there to Greece and Iran, it may be that the
myth of a spherical Primeval Man, which is justifiable, as
we have just seen, in the context of fifth-century Greek think-

[3] There is no need to suppose, as Götze tried to prove in 1923, that the
doctrine was borrowed by Greece from Iran: see J. D.-G. in *Harvard Theological Review* (1956), pp. 115 ff. On borrowings in the opposite direction, see J.
D.-G., "Quaestiones graeco-iranicae," *Klio* (1960), pp. 122–27.

ing, was similarly borrowed from the Greeks by the Iranians.

On the other hand, according to the Pahlavi Rivayat (127–137), the world is created from the body of a giant, but this text is apart, for Zaehner has shown (*Zurvan,* pp. 136ff.) that this narrative was borrowed from the famous Indian Purusa myth. This is evidently the case, as Zaehner has seen, with the slightly different doctrine which divides the body of man "between the four castes on earth: priesthood corresponded to the head, warriorhood to the hands, husbandry to the belly, and artisanship to the feet." In the first of the occurrences of this text explicit reference is made to foreign sources, Indian and Greek. The Indian origin is borne out by the passage in the Vedic hymn Rig Veda 10.90.12: "His mouth was the *Brahman;* his two arms were made the warrior; his two thighs the *vaishya;* from his two feet the *shudra* was born," a doctrine which became current in India.

However, a term occurring in the other Pahlavi version to describe man as *gehan i kotak,* which literally means "the small world," i.e. microcosm, seems to point to Greece. It is not at all excluded that borrowings from both quarters should have concurred in enriching the Iranian doctrine of the man-world relationship.

In the general frame of primitive thinking both the idea of a supreme god and that of man as a microcosm appear to result from a process of generalization. Taking into account Lévi-Strauss's considerations in *La Pensée Sauvage* (1962),[4] the microcosm idea may be said to be a particular case of man's projection on to his surroundings, namely, the extreme case in which these surroundings are embraced as

[4] And perhaps also of D.-G.'s on 'totality', *The Hymns of Zarathustra* (1952), Introduction.

a whole, as "the world." As for the supreme being, it also occupies an extreme position, namely, as the last link in the series of all the imaginable beings into which man could project himself.

There was a more typically and exclusively Iranian system of correspondences between God, man, and the world. It was represented in the series of *Amshaspands* or "Holy Immortal Ones" as patrons of "elements." This can be tabulated as follows:

Spenta Mainyu, "Holy Spirit"	Man
Vohu Manah, "Good Mind"	Ox
Aša Vahišhta, "Excellent Truth"	Fire
Xšhathra Vairya, "Desirable Dominion"	Metals
Haurvatat, "Wholesomeness"	Water
Ameretat, "Non-death"	Plants.

These Entities, which have been discussed in chapter one, can best be explained, together with the order in which they are arranged, by supposing, with Dumézil, that they corresponded to ancient Indo-Iranian gods who in turn were the patrons of the three functions of society: sovereignty (in its two forms, one more violent, the other more amiable or juridical), force or war, and health or prosperity. This yields the following picture (leaving aside Spenta Mainyu, who, being at the origin of everything, presided over the whole structure):

Mithra Varuna	Vohu Manah } Asha	Sovereignty	{ Ox Fire
Indra	Xshathra	War	Metals
the two Nasatyas	} Haurvatat { Ameretat	Prosperity	{ Water Plants

However, this social aspect of the picture, whether or not originally an integral part of it, was dropped in the course of time. We must admit that the Entities had ceased, in historical times, to be representative of the tripartite ideology. Already Zarathushtra, if he had inherited the doctrine, was less eager to distinguish between the functions than to subordinate them all to Ahura Mazda. Later on, in the later Avesta and in Pahlavi, the functions, or the classes that take them on, are symbolized, but it is not by means of the Amshaspands. Either it is through the haoma, the horse, and the ox (Yasna 11.1–6) or through colors (which is a very ancient piece of symbolism):[5] white for the priests, red or variegated for the warriors, and blue-black for the husbandmen; or yet again through legendary heroes like the three sons of Freton, or, finally, as in the two versions referred to above, through parts of the human body—to which the second of these versions, the *Shkand Gumanik Vicar,* chapter I, adds "the four virtues which are in man, namely temper, valor, wisdom, and energy. Unto temper is priesthood, as the greatest duty of priest is the temper that they do not commit sin on account of shame and fear; unto valor is warriorship, that is, the most princely adornment of warriors is the valor which is defined as self-possession; unto husbandmen is the wisdom which is strenuous performance of the tillage of the world to lead the world to the Renovation; unto artisans is energy which is the greatest advancement of their class." We shall have to say more on morals further below.

As for the *Amshaspands,* they retained a symbolic value, but it was something else they symbolized: either an analysis

[5] See above, p. 129.

of the material universe, through the objects of which they are the patrons, or a "psychology," as can be seen in 28.4 of the Great Bundahishn, in which Ohrmazd and the six *Amshaspands* are compared respectively to "the soul, intelligence, discernment, feeling, thought, knowledge, and explanation." On the other hand, they are assembled around Ohrmazd, according to chapter 26.8, in a manner which owes nothing to the tripartite ideology either: the first three, as males, on his right; the last three, as females, on his left; and Sraosha in front of him.

Another analysis provides another system of reference between man and his environment. The Avesta (Hadoxt Nask 2.15) teaches that the souls of the dead reach Paradise through three intermediate stages: *humata* (good thoughts), *huxta* (good words), and *hvarshta* (good deeds). Now, according to the Pahlavi books and the Sad Dar (a treatise in Persian), each of these stages is respectively identified with the place of the stars (the nearest to earth!), the moon, and the sun.

What is the reason for this order? It is obvious that the stars, moon, and sun follow each other in the order of increasing light, and this progression is completed in a fourth and final stage, which is the destination point of the soul's journey: one of the names of Paradise is, in fact, "Infinite Lights." That we have to do with a progression, a hierarchy, is moreover borne out by the fact that to each stage there corresponds a category of living beings: to the stars, the plants; to the moon, the animals; to the sun, man; to the Infinite Lights, the gods or God. Now, between these beings, the hierarchy is obvious: plants, animals, men, gods.

We thus have the following system:

Paradise	Infinite lights	God (or the gods)
Good deeds	The Sun	Man
Good words	The Moon	Animals
Good thoughts	The Stars	Plants

On the basis of certain indications, we are bound to believe that this doctrine was ancient, at least as old as the Avesta. In Avestan the moon is called *gao-cithra,* "having the race of the ox," and this means that the Avesta was familiar with the astrobiological belief, explicitly taught in the Pahlavi books, according to which the living species were preserved in the heavenly bodies: man in the sun, the animals in the moon, and the plants in the stars. (This accounted for the fixedness of the different species.) All this was told mythologically in the Bundahishn: at the death of Gayomart, the first man, a part of his seed fell onto the ground, while another part was collected by the god Neryosang, "messenger of humans," who took it to the sun to be purified. In the same way the seed of the Primordial Bull was borne to the moon. We shall return to this belief shortly, with reference to the fire doctrine, because the vital seed which transmits life, and hence warmth, is therefore a species of fire.

One of the most renowned ideas of Iranian civilization is the *Xvarenah,* which seems to lie at the origin of the aureoles of the saints of Buddhism, Christianity, and Islam. There is not enough space here[6] to explain the reasons which make it necessary to return, contrary to Bailey's thesis, to an etymology of the word *xvarenah* put forward about a hundred years ago, and which related it to *xvar* ("sun"), and hence to Sanskrit *svar* and its derivative *svarnara,* a term which seems

---

[6] See J. D.-G., *Annali dell' Istituto Orientale di Napoli* (1963), p. 19 ff.

to have designated the heavenly source of the soma, the sacred, invigorating liquor. So the *xvarenah* must be an emanation of the sun, the heavenly fire, a luminous life-force which is communicated to men. Now, this fluid is transmitted primarily to the head because, as Onians has ably demonstrated,[7] for the ancient Greeks, Latins, etc., this was the seat of vital power or strength. The figures (accompanied by the word φAPO or φAPPO) with a diadem and an aureole, which we find on certain Kushan coins, undoubtedly represent the same concept. We must nevertheless admit, in agreement with Bailey, the possibility of the transportation and transposition of attributes in a religion as obviously composite as that of the Kushans was.

But another type of portrayal of the *xvarr* (the Pahlavi form of *xvarenah*) was more sheltered from outside influences. It is the one appearing on the Sassanid coins, on which in general we find the expression of Mazdean orthodoxy. These are, specifically, certain coins of Ohrmazd II, of Shapur II, of Varhran V, and of Valash: on the fire altar a human head is shown, in the case of the first two in the flames of the altar, in the case of the other two, with no other flames but those radiating from the head itself. This figure is sometimes interpreted as being that of Ohrmazd, and we are referred in this respect to the Achaemenid reliefs. But on the latter Ahura Mazda is not *in* the fire: he hovers *above* the fire (when there is any fire shown), or rather, he dominates the entire scene, above the fire and the king. In the Sassanid portrayals, the head is on the altar, in the fire (or instead of it). So we can see in these, in agreement with Unvala (*Kharegat Memorial*

---

[7] *Origins of European Thought* (1953).

Volume, p. 52), "Fire" itself, the *Athsho* of the Kushan coins. One can even specify which fire: since the head is, in both cases, crowned, since these are royal coins, and since, as we have seen, the altar is sometimes given the appearance of a throne by the addition of lions' paws to it, we must come to the conclusion that this is the fire Varhran, the fire of kings and king of fires. Compare what we read in the Datastan i Denik: "when they see a fire in which there is Varhran." But if that is the case, another possibility arises. According to the evidence of Zatspram, the *xvarr* has its seat in the fire Varhran. So perhaps it was the *xvarr* that was meant to be portrayed. Must we, therefore, choose between these two interpretations: Atar or *Xvarr*? Perhaps they are not mutually exclusive: perhaps the intention was to portray, even more than the residence of one within the other, the fundamental oneness or identity of the heavenly fire, son of Ahura Mazda, and of the *Xvarenah,* the splendor that emanates from the sun to give men life and happiness.

That the nature of the *xvarenah* was both fiery and seminal is made abundantly clear by a number of texts, ranging from the Avesta to the Pahlavi writings. In order to prove this, we must first recall that, in the Iranian view, the essence of human and animal sperm was fire—accounting for animal warmth. We read in Great Bundahishn 17.4, that "the seed of men and animals is of the essence of fire," and in the same text, 22.2, that God created forth the sperm of men and animals from the light and verdure[8] of the sky, as these two sperms are of the essence of fire, not of water. Now Bailey, in his pioneer book *Zoroastrian Problems in the Ninth Century Books* (1943), p.

---

[8] I.e., its azure: like many peoples of Antiquity, the Iranians did not bother to distinguish between blue and green.

106, has seen in this a reflection of the Aristotelian doctrine according to which the *pneuma,* as basis of heat, consisting of matter related to the ether, enters the embryonic body with the sperm. But there is no exact correspondence between the two doctrines, which seem rather two independent representa tives of a primitive conception of fire as a life-force.

The conception of the fiery semen was probably already Indo-Iranian, for it is attested in Vedic India also, witness the ritual of the cosmic begetting performed by a Brahmin couple by means of two sticks of wood, one "feminine" and one "masculine." The fire-priest and his wife, he carrying the male stick, she the female one, sleep together. Their embrace generates the fire, which they produce on the follow-ing morning by means of the two sticks. This myth and ritual is justly compared by F. Herrmann, in his *Symbolik in den Religionen der Naturvölker* (1961), p. 149, with similar practices and beliefs among primitives. "At the death of a Ma Loango the state-fires are spent and the begetting of a new one is the first task of a new ruler. A couple especially chosen for this purpose, a youngster and a girl, must produce it by means of a 'man-wood' and a 'woman-wood.'" In a number of peoples there is some myth or other about the sexual origin of fire. Indeed, it may well be, as Bachelard contends,[9] that it was by imitating his sexual act with two dry sticks that man first invented fire!

It has been shown in chapter two that both Iran and Vedic India knew a system of correspondences between five kinds of fire and parts of the universe, ranging from the sky to plants and animals and man and woman. It is clear that at the base

[9] G. Bachelard, *Psychanalyse du Feu.*

of such a classification lies a primitive theory of the fiery nature of the vital fluid or sap which runs through the entire scale of beings. And here is undoubtedly still another reflection, which is very ancient, of the same theory: Apam Napat, a divinity certainly Indo-Iranian in date, and whose name literally means "grandson of the waters," is called in the Avesta (Yasht 19.52) "the god who created men (males), who fashioned men." Why specifically males, if not as the repositories of the fluid which transmits life and which originates in lightning? Such a theory will now enable us to explain the order in which material creation took place, namely: the sky, water, the earth, plants, cattle, and man. It is attested in the Bundahishn and alluded to in Denkart 278.7. Zaehner, in his latest book, *Dawn and Twilight of Zoroastrianism* (1961), p. 258, finds this order puzzling because it does not tally with the correspondences between the Entities and the material creation. But the reason why they differ is that the latter analyzes the world in its present state and, we may add, on the basis of the old socioreligious tripartition, whereas the other series is a genetic one, telling how the world was produced. Comparing the two orders, "the sky, for one thing," Zaehner writes, "has no counterpart among the Entities, whereas the metals, the counterpart of the Kingdom (which we have called Dominion), and, much more strangely, fire, the counterpart of Truth, do not appear among the original six creations at all." Now, the sky does not appear among the Entities because they *are* the sky, so to speak, or at least all of them are *in* it. Similarly, fire is absent from the "six original creations" because it is the very basis of them and is present in each of them. Here is how it works: fire, in the form of lightning, is in the *sky;* it comes down as rain—as a result, we may remem-

ber, of the fight between the Vazishta fire and the demon of
storm, Spenjagrya—in the form of *water,* which falls down on
to the *earth,* on which grow the *plants* containing *fire* (as
explained above); then fire passes into the *animals* and *man,*
both because they feed on plants and because of the fiery
semen which is the source of their animal warmth. As for the
metals, they have of course no place in this order because they
have no part to play in a process of life-development.

We can see now why the *Xvarenah* is at once a form of light
and a life-giving fluid: it amounts to the same thing. The
Xvarenah, described in the Avesta (Yasht 10.127) as "a blazing
fire" is said to be *awzhdatem* (Yasht 8.34), which means
"created (or put) in water." In the Karnamak legend referred
to above, p. 24, the *xvarr* of kingship is symbolized by a ram,
an animal famous for its procreative power. And why does
Ahura Mazda himself possess *xvarenah*? It is, according to
Yasht 19.10, "in order to create all creatures." Similarly,
Manushcihr in his Datastan, Question 36, speaks of "the intelligence and *xvarr* of the omniscient and almighty creator who
created the creatures." Again, in a detailed account given by
Denkart 347.10 ff. "concerning him who forms the *xvarr*" and
the whole process of creation, we can readily understand why
this life-giving fire is repeatedly stated to be "in the seed."
Zaehner's conclusion of his study of this passage (*Zurvan,* p.
371), that "the *xvarr* of God is simply his Being," is far too
abstract, and besides, Pahlavi had a word for "being" and this
was *hastih,* not *xvarr*. The *xvarr* of God is "simply" his seed.

The *xvarr*-light-life equation finally makes one passage in
the Bundahishn, (Great Bundahishn 164.13 ff.) perfectly clear
and intelligible. According to it, "the moon has to distribute
xvarr to the world; for fifteen days it waxes, for fifteen days

it wanes; it is like the sexual organ of males giving seed to females when it grows; thus the moon, too, in that manner, grows for fifteen days and dispenses happiness to the beings of the material world; it decreases for fifteen days, when it accepts duty and good deeds from those beings and consigns them to the treasure of God."

Another passage, Great Bundahishn 173.13–14, tells that Spendarmat (the Entity who is the patron of the earth) has for her allotted work the nourishment of the creatures, and also must see to it that "every evening a *xvarr* from each creation reverts towards Ohrmazd." This is probably an allusion to the ritual of the sacred fire, as we shall see presently.

In the Ritual

As we saw in chapter two, the rite of "feeding back" the domestic fire to the village fire every evening, then, periodically, the village fire to the provincial fire, and so on to the top of the hierarchy of fires, was a means of "enacting" the social symbolism of the fire cult. In so doing, all the fires were momentarily returned to their origin and lord, the Varhran fire. Alongside with the "sociopolitical" significance of the ritual, there seems to have existed a cosmic one, in that while everybody went to sleep at night, and the fires were covered with ashes for the night, "the *xvarr* from each creation," as the Bundahishn has it, was supposed to return to Ohrmazd in heaven.

The whole social order is also symbolized by the three fires corresponding to the three classes, *Farnbag* to the Priests, *Gushnasp* to the warriors, *Burzen-Mihr* to the husbandmen, plus the fire Varhran, pertaining unto the king. The king, in turn, symbolizes, if good, the Holy Spirit, but if bad, Ahriman (Denkart 401.3–5).

We also noted, Chapter II, several cosmic characteristics of the Yasna. The site of sacrifice symbolizes the world, with fire representing the sun, the table the earth, and the crescent-shaped stands the moon; the Yasna not only involved the use of fire, but also of water, metals, vegetal and animal elements; the parts into which the sacred bread was broken up recalled a cosmic pattern; the movement of the *raspi*, at a certain stage of the sacrifice, imitated that of the sun around the earth; the position of each of the seven priests is symbolic of the coming of the future saviors to each of the seven parts of the world; and proper orientation is essential. In this way the officiating priests can feel themselves, in the performance of the ceremony, firmly related not only to the gods but also to the cosmos.

Also, the structure of the sacred girdle is, as we saw, rich in cosmic allusions; and the flower ceremonies and the handclasp as well have a cosmic significance.

In the Ethics

The precepts of Mazdean ethics can be seen under two angles: maintenance of life and fight against evil. In order to maintain life one must earn one's living by means of cattle-raising and agriculture, and one must procreate. To fight against evil is to combat the demons and whatever beings, men or animals, belong to them. In a sense the two points of view seem to coincide, considering that the forces of evil are the forces of death: good is opposed to evil as light is to darkness, as life

to nonlife (Yasna 30.3). In fact, the life-precepts can be trans-
posed into fight-precepts: for instance, eating and drinking are
interpreted by Zatspram as a struggle against the she-demon Az
("Concupiscence").

In another sense, the two points of view are contradictory:
how can we fight the forces of evil without suppressing certain lives, for instance baleful animals? It is then the second
viewpoint that prevails: Iran ignores, even in theory, the
universal respect of life which is preached by Buddhism or
which justifies the vegetarian diet of Brahmanic India.

If human lives are at stake, which viewpoint will prevail?
Must one kill the enemies of life? On this point, Zoroastrianism varied. Zarathushtra urged that the forces of Lie should be
combated by force of arms. Under the Sassanids, from the
time of Karter onwards, Manichaeans, Christians, Buddhists,
etc. were persecuted. Under the Muslim rule, Mazdaism lost
all aggressiveness. There is only one case in which death is to
be preferred to life; that is when a Mazdean dies in order to
avoid apostasy. There remains the duty to treat the wicked
badly, a duty expressly proclaimed by Zarathushtra.

The "vitalistic" view-point contains, moreover, its own
condemnation: each living being feeds on another living
being, whom it must kill. And Aturpat, son of Mahraspand,
enjoins: "Abstain rigorously from eating the flesh of kine
and all domestic animals . . . for though you eat but a mouth-
ful, you involve your hand in sin, and though a camel be slain
by another man in another place it is as if you had slain it
with your own hand."[10] This interdiction is in line with
Zarathushtra's forbidding of at least some forms of the ox-

---

[10] Zaehner's translation in *The Teachings of the Magi* (1956), p. 111.

sacrifice. One could live on bread, milk, plants, and water, and one must in any case till the earth and raise cattle and milk it. Forsaking animal food will be the prelude to Resurrection. But Mazdaism in no case tolerates fasting, which is considered as weakening the faithful in their struggle against evil. And there are in the Avesta several references to animal food, perhaps a survival from nomadic times, when flesh was only eaten when it had been sacrificed.

Since sexual activity is subordinate to the duty of procreation, it is understandable that homosexuality should be banished, as well as intercourse with courtesans or prostitutes, personages who were typified in the Jeh, the Primeval Whore, whose action was interpreted in dualistic terms: she mixed up the seed of the wicked with that of the good, instead of keeping them apart.

It will also be seen that celibacy and absolute chastity are to be proscribed: the human kind ought to be perpetuated, as an indispensable auxiliary to Ohrmazd in his struggle against Ahriman. Mazdaism condemns the asceticism of the Christians, Manichaeans, etc.

It is less easy to see why adultery and polygamy should be condemned in the name of the same principle. On the contrary, if by indulging in a desire one stills it—as the demon of hunger is combatted by eating—this method should be authorized. In fact, Mazdak, the fifth-century "communist" reformer who claimed to interpret Zoroastrianism aright, recommended the sharing of women. Marriage—conjugal truthfulness—has owed its victory to social and economic reasons.

Social reasons also explain, it seems, the development of consanguineous marriage. This, according to the Rivayats, is nearly the most meritorious deed: it is only outranked by commission of all the rites to one priest. In the Rivayats it is a question of unions between first cousins, an interpretation also found in the Denkart. But it has not always been so. Gray's excellent study of the subject in the *Encyclopaedia of Religion and Ethics,* VIII, 456, is worth being summarized: the Avesta mentions *xvaetvadatha* in five passages only, all of them recent, and without defining the term. Zarathushtra ignores it. Greek and Latin authors notice marriage between parents and children or between uterine brothers and sisters, not only in the royal family of Persia but with the Persians generally, and particularly with the Magians. The use is continued in Sassanid times. The Pahlavi texts warmly recommend it and leave no doubt as to its definition. In the Denkart its origin is justified by the will to preserve the purity of the race, and to increase the chances of mutual understanding between consorts and affection for their children. The Pahlavi Rivayat remarks—perhaps rightly, given the Muslim rule— that exogamy might foster religious laxity and even apostasy. A usage more recommended than observed, it seems to have been alien to Zarathushtra's doctrine, but it was perhaps an old Indo-European practice, for it had its counterpart amongst the Old Prussians and Lithuanians, who permitted marriage with a parent (except the mother), and amongst the ancient Irish. In Iran it seems that the Magians tried to impose "this extreme form of endogamy" (Gray) under the Sassanids and in the first centuries of Muslim rule.[10a] But it was resisted by the mass of the faithful and has disappeared.

Distributive justice was regulated from on high by the

[10a] It is proved by a recently published Pahlavi text, the *Rivayat i Hemit i Ashavahishstan* (1962), to have really been practised in medieval Iran.

principles of veridicalness and respect of contracts. A salary that has been promised must be paid, says Zarathushtra. More particularly, hoarding and usury are condemned in the Rivayats as grave faults. A just interest is permissible (Sad Darband Hosh 38).

Zatspram disapproves of covetousness and avarice. To be charitable is a source of merits: "He who will give (to a faithful one) a quantity of meat equal to this bird of mine Parodarsh (the cock)," says Ahura Mazda (Videvdat 18.29), "I shall not question him twice on his entering Paradise." It is even a duty, for the one who refuses even a very small part of his wealth to a just one who is asking for it, makes pregnant the she-demon of Lie, "as the other males make the females pregnant by laying their seed into them" (*ibidem*, 34).

The interests of religion are those of the establishment: religious law dominates, at least theoretically, the whole life (as in Islam). Artaxsher the Sassanid king is supposed to have said that religion and kingship are brothers, none of which can do without the other. Religion is the foundation of kingship, and the latter protects the former. Now, whatever lacks foundation must perish and whatever lacks a protector vanishes away. It is important for the good march of the world that everybody should keep his place, viz., accomplish the duties of his class (Denkart 45.15–19 and Letter of Tosar).

The economic order, threatened by the "communist" preachings of Mazdak, was restored by a king, Khosrau Anosharvan. What the Evil Spirit mostly fears is the union into one person of kingship and the good religion (Denkart 129). In fact, at the end of time, the work of the Saviors will be preluded by that of a king, Varhran the Splendid.

A theory of virtues and vices is sometimes found with the

Iranian moralists, for instance, the one studied by Father de Menasce,[11] which recalls to us a well-known Greek model, the *Ethics to Nicomachus.* Menasce compares several passages, which he designates with letters and the doctrine of which he summarizes as follows: "Text A, dealing with the repression of vice, points out that it must not entail the suppression of the virtues which the vices resemble. In B, the formula requires that the virtues should be pure of any mingling with the vices which, according to C, seek to supplant them. The health of the soul implies therefore an exact measure insuring the adjustment of the powers, and safeguards them from the intrusion of antagonistic elements that would alter them."

This doctrine presupposes another one, namely that of the Mean (*patman*), which Iran vindicates as its own—as Islam does as well: "Iran has always lauded just measure and blamed excess and default," says Denkart 429.11. "Amongst the Byzantines the philosophers, in India the scholars, and elsewhere the specialists have in general praised the man with a subtle speech, but the realm of Iran has approved the sages." In fact, it is difficult to decide whether it was a borrowing from Aristotle or a genuinely Iranian notion. It may be of use to remark, at all events, that the Chinese had also their Doctrine of the Mean.[12]

This notion collided in Iran with a cosmogonic notion designated by the same term of *patman*, namely, the pact concluded between Ohrmazd and Ahriman to fight each other during a limited number of years—a formula of nonpeaceful coexistence!

---

11 *Une Encyclopédie Mazdéenne* (1958), p. 39.
12 See J. P. Bruce, *Chu Hsi and His Masters,* p. 217, quoted by Brandon, *Man and his Destiny* (1962), p. 370.

Anyhow, as a maxim it does not belong to a rough or primitive nation, but to a civilized one, capable of mild mores like those advocated by Aturpat, son of Mahraspand, who writes: "Do not harbor vengeance in your thoughts lest your enemies catch up with you. Consider rather what injury, harm, and destruction you are liable to suffer by smiting your enemy in vengeance and how you will (perpetually) brood over vengeance in your heart."[13] This is a far cry from Zarathushtra's preaching holy war and enjoining to treat the wicked badly!

Ethics finally soars up to the notion of disinterestedness: "Do good," says Aturpat, "simply because it is good." Man's destiny depends of the choice he makes each moment, and in the smallest details of his life, between truth and lie, between good words, thoughts, and deeds, and evil ones. And this choice is free. Zarathushtra already said so, and there is in Pahlavi a term for those "whose will is free": *azad-kam*.[14]

How are we to explain that, as often happens, the just are unhappy? How can fate's omnipotence be reconciled with the freedom of the will? The Mazdeans have asked themselves the question. Their most striking solution is that expressed in the Pahlavi Videvdat: *gete pat baxt, menok pat kunishn* ("the material is according to fate, the spiritual according to action"); in other words, we depend on fate only for the material things, whereas in the spiritual order our action is autonomous. The Iranians may have found this formula unaided. Nevertheless, it cannot be ignored that the Neo-

[13] Zaehner, *The Teachings of the Magi*, p. 110.
[14] Jackson's study, "The Zoroastrian Doctrine of the Freedom of the Will," *Zoroastrian Studies*, pp. 219 ff., must be supplemented and corrected by means of that of Tavadia, *Zeitschr. f. Indologie u. Iranistik*, VIII, 119 ff.; see also Zaehner, *Zurvan*, p. 254 and texts Z 33, etc.

Platonists had found a similar one, at least as far as the content is concerned. They had found this means to "escape determinism," as we would say: they identified the *heimarmene* to the *physis,* and so left the soul free. However, if the Iranians may have been attracted by this formula, they did not borrow it as it was. Plotinus used to say that the soul, when without the body, is free. The Iranians, unless they were Manichaeans, did not despise matter, and thought little of the soul separated from it.

This conception safeguarded human responsibility by limiting the efficacy of human endeavor to the moral domain, the *menok* sphere, future life. But, as it was, it was too hard, and in practice it underwent two compromises. On the one hand, it appeared superhuman to abandon all things of this world to a Fate on which one had no grip. Was it really not possible in the material domain to influence fate? It must be in certain cases. The gods must be swayed. In order to sustain such a hope a distinction was drawn in the Pahlavi books between *baxt,* which is simply fate—which even the gods cannot change—and *bagobaxt,* which is "fate allotted by the gods," who remain able to modify it according to the prayers or merits of everyone.[15]

On the other hand, future life should be determined by the balance of the good and evil deeds, words, and thoughts of the whole life: this principle is propounded in all its strictness, so much so that a special dwelling-place—*hamestagan*—is provided for those whose good deeds exactly balance their evil ones. In fact, this principle also is tempered to allow for human weakness. All of the faults do not have to be registered

[15] See Zaehner, *Zurvan,* pp. 254 ff.

or weigh forever in the scales. There are two means of effacing them. One is confession, with contrition and penance: "I have made this penance," says the Patet-formula translated by Zaehner (*Teachings*, p. 123), "in order to wipe out my sins, obtain my share of reward for good deeds done, and for the comfort of my soul," etc. The second means is the transfer of supererogatory merits (the equivalent of the Christian "Communion of Saints"): "Should it happen to me that I leave this world without having done my [final] penance and someone from among my near relations should do penance on my behalf, I agree to it." This transfer of merits is the justification of the prayers and ceremonies for the dead; but these are deemed efficacious of themselves, independently of the merits of those who perform or sponsor them. These rites can be performed in the lifetime of the beneficiary, whether he is or not considered *in articulo mortis*. According to the Sad Darband Hosh, one may have sinned much: if the rites have been performed *in articulo mortis* the soul at the moment of death, when passing the Bridge of the Requiter, is assisted by "the Spirit of the Gathas," who supports her and prevents her from falling into hell and into the hands of Ahriman. As to the ceremony performed when one is not *in articulo mortis*, its advantages are subject to a tariff: it is, namely, seven hundred times more profitable to have the Yasna performed, not in a discontinued way, but by four priests taking turns two by two for three days and three nights.

Mazdaism is therefore not the purely moral religion it may seem.[16] And even the picture we have sketched is still likely

[16] Cf. Jackson, *Zoroastrian Studies*, p. 138: "The ideal picture must not be overdrawn"; and Lehmann, *Enc. Rel. & Eth.*, V, 515: "The reverse of this ethic is an abstract stiffness that will not accommodate itself to life, and whose

to be deceptive, owing to the stress put on free choice. In practice the Mazdean is constantly involved in such a meticulous struggle against the contamination of death and a thousand causes of defilement, against the threat, even in his sleep, of ever-present demons, that he should not often feel to be leading his life freely, morally.

Aside from this Mazdean attitude, the belief in the power of destiny sometimes exasperates itself into fatalism. This is a major theme and spring of the Epics. Fatalism easily associates itself with Zurvanism, itself sometimes tainted with material-ism. And we read in the Menok-i-Xrat that "though one be armed with the valor and strength of wisdom and knowledge, yet it is not possible to strive against fate. For once a thing is fated and comes true, whether good or the reverse, the wise man goes astray in his work, and the man of wrong knowledge becomes clever in his work; the coward becomes brave, and the brave cowardly; the energetic man becomes a sluggard and the sluggard energetic. For everything that has been fated a fit occasion arises which sweeps away all other things."[17]

But it remains true, on the whole, as Zaehner writes,[18] that "the theological premisses" of Mazdaism "are based on an essentially moralistic view of life."

---

irrational consequences are often inimical to life. The monotonous opposition of good to evil and evil to good leaves no room for the intermediate stages of real life, for the individual and spontaneous states in the soul of man. The Persians cared little for the emotions of disinterestedness; even in the religious feelings we feel too often the want of lyric elements; on the contrary, we always feel the burden of the juristic spirit."

[17] Translated by Zaehner, *Zurvan*, p. 257.
[18] *Teachings of the Magi*, p. 97.

V

Mazdaism and Sufism

Mazdaism survived in a subtle fashion in the Sufi literature, verse and prose. The motifs of metaphors which allude to it in the works of the Sufi poets have recently been studied by Muhammad Mu'in in a Persian book bearing the title *"Mazdean influence in Persian literature."* The chief object of this work, as Henry Corbin says in a thirty-six-page French summary, is to study the "ideograms" or "ciphers" by which the Sufi poets endeavor to typify in Mazdean reminiscences their nostalgia for a free, spiritual religion transcending the official religious Law." But Bausani, in his recent book *La Persia religiosa* (Rome, 1960), has established a different perspective by distinguishing on the one hand a Mazdean thematic form, which is purely verbal and goes back to Firdousi and the other epic poets, and on the other hand, Gnostic and Neo-Platonic contents deriving from the "great Hermetico-Pythagorean, and then Neo-Platonic importations through Arabic translations of the eighth to tenth centuries. The combination of those two themes may have produced the illusion of a direct derivation from Mazdaism."

The most important of those symbols[1] is the Wine of the
Magi: wine forbidden by Islam and used in the Mazdean
liturgy, suggested deliverance from the commandments of
orthodoxy, as well as a means of ecstasy. Wine had, according
to tradition, been invented by Jamshid, an epic reminiscence.
Since it is in Jamshid's cup that one drinks the beverage
revealing the secret of things, its roundness reflects the sphere
of the world, etc. (Corbin, apud Mu'in, p. 33 passim, proposes
to translate it by "the Grail").[2] To wine and the cup are
associated the Tavern and the cup-bearer, which may also be
called respectively Fire-Temple and Son of the Magi, even
as the Magus glimmers behind the "wine-drinker."[3] The old
one or "Ancient" of the Magi, another symbol, represents the
Perfect Man, a distantly Mazdean conception transmitted by
the Gnostic movement. And the Convent of the Magi is,
still more mystically, the "World of the divine Names, first
stage for the soul on her way to perfection."[4]

These various symbols have been studied by Mu'in in the
erfani poets, who use them constantly: Sana'i (11th–12th C.),
for whom Mazdeans and Sufis are the same people, professing
one mystical religion of love; 'Attar of Nishapur, who claims:
"We are the eternal Mazdeans, we are not Muslims!";
Mawlawi (d. 1273); Faxreddin of Hamadan, alias 'Iraqi (13th

---

[1] Bausani writes, p. 303, that it is in the Arab poetry of the first centuries
of Islam that the origin of these symbols (perhaps less mystical and esoteric
than sometimes contended) should be sought.

[2] Bausani remarks, p. 304, that not until the twelfth century was the cup
attributed to Jamshid and only then because that personage was identified
with Solomon; on the other hand, he further observes, the cup motif belonged
less to ancient Iran than to the Hellenistic and Gnostic world.

[3] According to Bausani, p. 327, this Temple has nothing to do with the
Mazdean cult.

[4] Corbin, apud Mu'in, p. 32.

C.); Hafiz (d. 1389); Hatif of Ispahan (d. 1784). Moreover, Mu'in has culled the slightest Mazdean reminiscences in all the great poets of Iran, from Daqiqi (10th C.) to Jami through Firdousi, Asadi of Tus (author of the *Garshasp nama*), Gorgani (adaptator of the Parthian poem *Vis o Ramin*), Nasir-i-Khosrau, Nizami, Xaqani, Sa'di, 'Unsuri, and has devoted a detailed monography to Zartusht Bahram, the author of the *Zartusht nama* and other strictly Mazdean poems.

A parallel study on the philosophers has been initiated by Horten and is pursued by Henry Corbin, chiefly about Sohravardi.[5] Sohravardi, who died in 1191, felt or wished himself the heir of both Greece and Iran. He bases his philosophy on "the doctrine of the Orientals, i.e., of the Persian Magi asserting two sources, one of which is Light, the other Darkness."[6] But the opposition of these two sources is interpreted peripatetically: "That is in effect a symbol of Necessity and Possibility."

Light is often designated by one or two typically Zoroastrian terms: *Xorra*, i.e., the royal and divine splendor (Pahlavi *Xvarr*), and *ray*, an almost synonymous term but which the first commentators of Sohravardi seem no longer to have understood. Thus Qotb-addin Shirazi explains this

[5] Horten, *Die Philosophie der Erleuchtung nach Suhrawardi* (1912); *Die philosophische Systeme der speculativen Theologie im Islam* (1912); *Die Philosophie des Islam* (1924). — Corbin's theses are developed in *Les motifs zoroastriens dans la philosophie de Sohravardi* (Teheran, 1946), in the *Prolegomena* to his edition of the *Oeuvres philosophiques et mystiques de Sohravardi*, I (Istanbul, 1945), II (Teheran, 1952), and in various contributions to the *Eranos-Jahrbücher*. See also Corbin, *L'Imagination créatrice dans le soufisme d'Ibn 'Arabi* (Paris, 1958). — Bausani, pp. 181 ff. studies the Iranian elements in the *Ummu 'l Kitab*.

[6] *Opera Metaphysica et Mystica*, II, Appendix, p. 301, gloss 13; in Corbin's translation, p. 24.

word as the singular of the Arabic word *ara'*. Corbin wonders how the commentators can have lost sight of the "Avestic significance of the word *ray*" and concludes: "The use made of it by Sohravardi in joining *xorra* and *ray* in a correct and characteristic manner suggests that he had direct access to certain authentic sources, written or oral." The sources in question are not far to seek. Both terms are used together in the most current phrase of Mazdaism, a Pahlavi phrase which was pronounced when beginning any action (writing, among others), and which appears to have been copied from the Muslim *bismi 'llah*. Here it is: *pa nam i rayomand i xvar-romand*. Knowledge of this phrase represented indeed a minimum of acquaintance with Zoroastrianism. What is surprising, then, is that the commentators of our philosopher should have forgotten its meaning. Or rather: was it not always the commentators' task to turn their backs on the obvious and seek something else?

This glorious light gives birth to beings called *anwar qahira*, a term to which Corbin finds a Zoroastrian flavor and which he proposes, after some groping, to translate by *lumières victoriales*. I think the allusion is even more precise than he believes: *anwar qahira* seems indeed to transpose in the plural *Atash Bahram* and to refer, therefore, to the major fires of the Mazdean nation—an adequate designation of a celestial hierarchy.

Sohravardi knows the names of the Amshaspands, amongst whom he gives Bahman the first rank, which is in accord with the Mazdean doctrine. But these Amshaspands derive from the light of glory through a procession which recalls, on the contrary, that of the hypostases in the Greek systems. This mixture cannot be wondered at if one remembers it was already attested in Mazdaism, namely, in the fourth book of the Denkart.[7]

The scheme of procession is, in any case, very complicated in Sohravardi's thought, compared with that of Avicenna, for example. Sohravardi distinguishes three series of hypostases: the first one constitutes the world of "Mothers," transcendent beings, absolutely separate (in the Gnostic sense); the second one is the order of the archangels-theurges, archetypal persons or Lords of the Species; the third is that of the Angels-Souls, energies moving the celestial orbs or the human creatures.

Now, the Amshaspands do not all belong to one series, but to two. Bahman alone is part of the first one, in the world of "Mothers"; the other Amshaspands, ruling, as in Mazdaism, over the various provinces of the universe, are classified amongst the Lords of the Species: *Esfandarmoz* (angel of the Earth), *Ordibehešt* (of Fire), *Xordad* and *Mordad* (of water and plants). This is a break, a quartering, as Corbin says, in the primitive series of Entities, which is revealing for the liberty Sohravardi takes with his Iranian sources. This touches upon a question of principle with which we shall deal briefly. But we may first note, to close the chapter of Mazdean terms, the name of the energies of the third order: they are called lights-*espahbads*. In Pahlavi literature the word *spahpat* ("general, commander") is applied to the signs of the zodiac around Ohrmazd and the planets around Ahriman.[8]

What was the relative importance of the Zoroastrian element in Sohravardi's thought and his faithfulness to his Mazdean sources?[9] We should insist on the fact, already

[7] J. de Menasce, *Une Encyclopédie mazdéenne: le Dēnkart* (1958), p. 23.

[8] Menok-i-Xrat, 8; cited in Corbin, p. 45.

[9] Bausani, p. 241 ff., shows that Sohravardi's "Mazdean" ideas are tinged with Manichaeism.

mentioned above, that the Sohravardian synthesis had already been adumbrated in the Mazdean tradition, which had absorbed the Greek doctrine of the procession of hypostases in order to interpret the series of the Entities. Can Sohravardi then have believed that his philosophy, drawing from two sources, reflected each of them exactly? He may have believed he carried on both of them, because he found the truth in both. Objectivity is easier to a nonbeliever. But, between a scholar who tries to reconstruct a manner of thinking which remains foreign to him, and a mystic philosopher who is moved by it and makes it his own—which of the two may be said better to secure its survival? Sohravardi, as he placed himself in the double lineage of Iran and Greece, did not proceed otherwise than the Greeks of late antiquity who claimed to descend from Pythagoras and, through him, from Zoroaster. When they believed they were gaining access to eternal truth, they were in fact renewing human thought. And indeed the Zoroastrian heritage, piously transmitted and copied through the centuries, never experienced any renewal comparable to the Sohravardian reorientation.

For Mazdaism, from the tenth-century catastrophe onwards, seems to have had only the strength to survive, not to renew itself. What marks its development from then on, and constitutes in a way its history, is the shocks of its encounters with different worlds: first Islam, then India, finally Europe. As a further test: when Mazdeans have dealings with other Mazdeans—the Parsee immigrants in India with the Gabars who remained in Iran—nothing new takes place.

Index